D1296108

A River's Pleasure:
Essays in Honor of John Cronin

Pace University Press • New York

A River's Pleasure:

Essays in Honor of John Cronin

Edited by

Michelle D. Land
Pace University Academy for Applied
Environmental Studies

and

Susan Fox Rogers
Bard College

Pace University Press
2009

Table of Contents

The book cover and table of contents were designed by Sasha Harris-Cronin, who has been collaborating with John Cronin for nearly thirty-four years as both daughter and designer. Among other projects, they have worked together on graphic designs for the Hudson Fisheries Trust and the Pace Academy for the Environment. She works in San Francisco creating interactive exhibits for museums throughout the country.

FOREWORD

Thirty-five years seems like a long time. That is, unless you happen to be older than thirty-five and reading this. Then, I am sure, it seems difficult to account for it—years slip into one another, months ratchet by without regard to natural order, holidays are a blur, and significant moments stand aloft like the tips of tall pines that tower, here and there, over the rest of your forested time on earth.

Of course, in the context of the Hudson River Valley that period barely registers at all. Given a consciousness like our own, the river would probably feel it as a half-thought, not even fully articulated, passing so briefly as not to interrupt the flow of its estuarial mind.

And to John Cronin this period must feel somewhere between a half-thought and a fully-dedicated life mission well-lived. For him, it represents the portion of his adult life focused on the mission that is celebrated in this book. It represents the period of his perseverance on the issues of environmentalism and more specifically the Hudson River, which found him, plucked him from its shores, and put him to work on its behalf. In contemplating how this relationship came about, I imagine the Hudson must have watched John's youth, liked something about his aimless vacillations punctuated by passionate decision points, and figured that he was the perfect combination of arrogance, brilliance, charm, and ingenuity to help collaborate on its resurgence. So the meeting was arranged and John met the river he had known about but not understood for twenty-some years, and they got to work.

As we who live in its valley or love it from a distance fully understand, the Hudson is a complex river whose ancient origins, biological complexity, historical significance, and leading role as an environmental touchstone are well-known and well-deserved. Its complexity makes it truly unique, and it therefore naturally required a bevy of complex characteristics for its partnership with John.

Happily, John fulfills those characteristics with vigor, since his career on the Hudson is the product of profound contradictions: a landlubber who learns to fish from multi-generation fishermen; a political neophyte who begins by writing legislation; an informally-appointed surveyor who becomes an official enforcer; a suspicious interviewer who becomes a litigious investigator; a thinker unencumbered by an advanced degree awarded one honorifically and now dedicating his life to that educational enterprise.

In all of the episodes of his career dedicated to the Hudson and environmental issues John has maintained the passion and persistence to carry them onward. But now—and in my view much more significant—John adds to them a sense of perspective gained from his thirty-five years engaged in this mission. To that he adds the invaluable and extensive network of partners committed to moving environmental understanding of the Hudson and other rivers and estuaries to the forefront of our thinking as a society, some of whom share their thoughts in the pages that follow. John embodies a remarkable breadth of understanding wrought from real-world experience and deep connections among the scholarly, legislative, activist, residential and commercial interests that bind themselves to the Hudson River.

This book is an overview of that breadth by authors brought together to muse on the subject of John's last thirty-five years, to celebrate the contradictory ebb and flow of the events during that time, to collect some of our thinking by the Hudson and for the Hudson, in the environment and about the environment, about issues that intersect the subject, and about the curious and wonderful relationship between John and the river.

In his great poem "A Scene on the Banks of the Hudson" (1827)—my personal favorite of all poems about the river— William Cullen Bryant ends with an apostrophe to the river, outlining the moment in time when one person, after having looked into the depths of the Hudson and seen his own world mirrored there, turns back to engage with the world. "River," he writes:

Thy fate and mine are not repose,
And ere another evening close,
Thou to thy tides shalt turn again,
And I to seek the crowd of men.

This contemplative and interactive relationship—this intellectual, physical and spiritual symbiosis—is the essence of what we need to pursue in this remarkable river valley and across the globe now more than ever. Like Bryant before him, John has reminded us for thirty-five years that our lives and livelihoods depend upon it.

Geoffrey L. Brackett
Provost and Executive Vice President for Academic Affairs,
Pace University

INTRODUCTION

I. History

This publication might just as easily have taken the form
of a banquet dinner. Allow me to explain. In February 2008,
during a private meeting with John Cronin, I mentioned that
I wished to publicly acknowledge his thirty-five years in the
environmental advocacy field. Never before had I contemplated
the options for honoring someone whose accomplishments were
as multifaceted as John's. So, rather uncreatively, I admit, I
suggested that perhaps we would have a dinner event to celebrate
his achievements. I now know there was a slight panic stirring
in his thoughts at that moment. Having explained that I would
be doing *something* to honor him and it would be better to have
his cooperation than not, John quickly took to the task of finding
alternatives to the dinner notion. Fortunately for all of us, he
consulted with his friend, and my colleague, Susan Fox Rogers,
who offered this elegant idea of a compilation of essays from
those who have influenced—and have been influenced by—John
Cronin's career.

It is important for us to share that it took a significant
amount of convincing for John to be agreeable with our honoring
his life's work. What most people don't realize is that John is
an intensely private individual. While he is savvy in the public
relations and communications arena, John is by no means
comfortable being in the spotlight, especially if his life is the topic.
As such, this endeavor was conceived of and is being executed
entirely by John's colleagues; John is an innocent bystander.
Thus, although he was generally kept apprised of the progress,
John was not directly involved; in fact we all agreed that he
wouldn't even see the essays until the book was in print. There
is no question, however, that he is deeply and immeasurably
heartened by the fact that the authors herein thought enough of
him to contribute.

This publication is a fitting way to pay tribute to John's
work because literature and writing are central to his life—one
of his greatest passions. The contributing authors are multi-

disciplinary because, like John's own career, we wanted to contemplate, portray and reflect upon the many facets of the complex interrelationship between humans and nature. We encouraged the authors to write about their own thinking that has been either shaped by John or was otherwise connected to John's perspective. There is no question that scores of potential contributors are missing from this book—we acknowledge their omission and offer our apologies with the explanation that there is simply not enough time in a day (or in one and one-half years) to corral all who would want to share their own story. Perhaps we'll all get together for dinner some day.

II. Organization

A note on the organization of the pages that follow: The order of essays is based loosely on a timeline of when the author first intersected with John. Years reflected in the table of contents do not necessarily match up precisely with the initial interaction, but they are in close range. The book is ordered in this fashion to provide an added layer of history to the chronicle of John's career. Chronology allows the reader to gain a sense of how John's thinking has evolved and how he and the contributors reciprocally impacted each other along the way.

III. Content

As Geoffrey L. Brackett so eloquently states in the Foreword, "John embodies a remarkable breadth of understanding wrought from real-world experience and deep connections among the scholarly, legislative, activist, residential and commercial interests that bind themselves to the Hudson River." Indeed, John's breadth of understanding and interests are evident throughout this book and its authors' unique perspectives.

John's environmental work began in 1973 as a volunteer the Hudson River Sloop Clearwater. In 1974, John joined the Pipewatch staff, under the direction of the first riverkeeper, Tom Whyatt. In an interview with Susan Fox Rogers, Pete Seeger recounts his first meeting with John and gives us a glimpse of how John's apparent aimlessness at the time was transformed by his simple offer to help a stranger repair a dock.

Not long after that fateful day on the Beacon dock, John's career as an environmental advocate attracted the attention of then *Poughkeepsie Journal* reporter, Jim Detjen. In the summer of 1974, Detjen (a new reporter on the scene) accompanies John on an environmental adventure investigating Tuck Tape Industries and its illegal discharges from twenty-seven different pipes. Once the case was won in 1975 and the *Poughkeepsie Journal* published the story, each of their careers was launched—John's as an environmental activist, organizer, and educator; and Detjen's as an investigative environmental journalist. Detjen remembers how in those days they were both "young, idealistic, and without much money."

Anyone who has spent even five minutes with John probably knows that water protection is his calling. In the mid-1970's, John began what was to become a long, productive and meaningful friendship with Nicholas Robinson, then a young practicing attorney in the nascent field of environmental law. Robinson's thinking can be heard in John's words today about the urgent need to update our water laws (namely the Clean Water Act) and in particular increase standards of these obsolete statutes. Robinson's essay explains how citizen engagement will be a critical tool as we urge our state and federal governments to protect the nation's waters and hydrologic cycle by re-examining our laws, properly applying regulations currently in place and contemplating an amendment to the Constitution to include an environmental provision.

In the late 1970's, John was a district project coordinator for Congressman Hamilton Fish, Jr., and then a legislative aide to New York State Assemblyman Maurice Hinchey and the Assembly Environmental Conservation Committee. During this time in government, John's assignments included drafting coastal management legislation and the investigation of the U.S. Army's role in Love Canal while exposing Manhattan Project contractors who had pumped radioactive wastes into the drinking water aquifers. Paul Bray, an attorney and legislative draft writer, along with Congressman Hinchey, have co-written a succinct yet thorough review of environmental policy in New York State and in particular the Congressman's role in shaping it. Bray and Hinchey recall the Love Canal investigation and how John's dedication to the research meant that at times he would sleep on the couch in Hinchey's office. They note that early on Congressman Hinchey recognized the story behind pollution "involves many villains but a considerable amount of the environmental damage that has been done to our planet is simply a result of ignorant, under-regulated, or careless industrial activity."

One of the many reasons John is a highly respected environmental advocate in the Hudson Valley is that he worked on the front lines as a Hudson River commercial fisherman for two years, from 1980—1982. John learned the trade from Hudson rivermen who were guardians of the indigenous knowledge of this ancient occupation. Fishing and the River defined these men, creating an iconic culture that has all but disappeared. John transcribed and edited a conversation with Henry Gourdine (1903–1997), a dedicated, skilled fisherman and Hudson River legend, into an oral history, "Duty Bound." Even as Gourdine recalls making less than $25 a week at times (in the 1920s), he clearly loved his profession, saying, "If I had it all to do over again, I don't regret any of the time. I would start right over again, I would still be a fisherman." His professional fishing career spanned seventy-seven years. Gourdine talks of a fellow fisherman, Tucker Crawford, who would say to Gourdine, "You know, Henry…It's too bad that someone in your family hasn't taken it up too like building a boat, and rigging the nets and fishing the nets, and understand the different types of gear. It's a sad occasion. First, to accumulate the knowledge that you have over the years, and then you're not able to pass it on anywhere." Though John no longer fishes, passing on information about the river—teaching others—has been at the heart of his work.

Perhaps known most widely for his role as the Hudson Riverkeeper, John held the post from 1983–2000. It was then that he co-founded the Pace Law School Environmental Litigation Clinic and in 1984 met Robert (Bobby) Kennedy, Jr., co-author of the book *The Riverkeepers*. In his essay, Kennedy reminisces about their days in the trenches, crawling up pipes to take samples and stakeouts in the dark to catch midnight dumpers. Kennedy reminds us that John's position on environmental protection is guided by his deep connection to community, "He saw human beings as part of the landscape he sought to protect, and he saw the Hudson as a community—where sports fisherman, commercial fisherman, river pilots, oil tankers, barges, and pleasure boats might enjoy the bounties of Creation and support their livelihoods." Indeed, among John's primary motivating beliefs is that access to the river is a human right.

In an illuminating and insightful essay, Alex Wilkinson describes his first profile for *The New Yorker* in 1987, the subject of which was John Cronin. Wilkinson reaches beyond the usual content of John's curriculum vitae to tell the story of a more colorful life that included a scholarship to Hartford Ballet Company; living in a car in a junkyard; and a door-to-door salesman job with a book company. Wilkinson takes us through the journey of John's career, peeling away the layers to reveal John's core: his restlessness, continual reinvention, and a never-ending source of big ideas, most of which *do* come to fruition.

While serving as the Hudson Riverkeeper, John Cronin inspired a legacy of more than 160 Waterkeeper programs on six continents, including the NY/NJ Baykeeper, which launched in 1989. The International Waterkeeper Alliance was conceived of by Andrew Willner (NY/NJ Baykeeper) and John, while both John and Bobby Kennedy "midwifed it into reality in 1999." Recently retired, Willner admits in his essay that he didn't grow up loving the bays of New York Harbor. He learned how to care by observing the wildlife that depend on its ecosystem and protecting his daughter from the nearby "needle beach" in Staten Island. Willner came to realize that Baykeepers are first responders for water protection as the "hard core advocates" who fight "David and Goliath battles." But he also acknowledges that the battles alone are not enough; the Keeper programs must also be pro-active problem solvers.

George Ancona, photographer and author of children's books, has had his work published in over 100 books. Through his book, Ancona strives to open up the world to children. In his contribution to this compilation, he shares photographs and accompanying text excerpted from a few of his publications, namely: *Turtle Watch* (1987); *Man and Mustang* (1992); and *The Golden Lion Tamarin Comes Home* (1994). In his photography and writing, Ancona profiles people who are working to make a difference. Among his subjects was John Cronin in the book, *Riverkeeper* (1990). On his website[1] Ancona appropriately describes John as a man who "wears many hats. He is an environmentalist, an activist, an orator, a fisherman, and even a detective—all in his role as caretaker of the Hudson River." Perhaps the most important message conveyed by Ancona in his book is that "John loves his work....Make your interests your career—and enjoy it."

Given the philosophical influence on John Cronin by Trappist monk Thomas Merton[2] (1915–1968) and passionist priest Thomas Berry[3] (1914–2009), it is not surprising that John would befriend an academically inclined Episcopal priest and anthropologist. In this lovely piece, Rev. Jeffrey Golliher relives his first meeting with John at a café near Grand Central Station a decade or so ago. "We both understood that building an ecologically rooted sense of community was at the heart of our vocation; yet, 'the world' seemed to be moving in the opposite direction. The difference between the two and the struggle we had with it—and probably still have—was the reason for our meeting." Golliher goes on to say "Everyone has a vocation to heal our broken relation with the Earth whether or not we're fortunate enough to live it as our 'job.'"

In an intriguing intermission from the water and river themes, John Horgan discusses in his essay the question of whether humanity will (can?) stop fighting wars. Horgan and John are Cold Spring, New York neighbors and we learn that in typical fashion, they are not on the same side of the debate—

---

[1] George Ancona, Children's Books, http://www.georgeancona.com (accessed August 9, 2009).

[2] John Cronin was a 2006-2007 International Merton Society Shannon Fellow at Bellarmine University where he researched and wrote about "The Ecological Theology of Thomas Merton: A Model for the 21st Century."

[3] John received the Thomas Berry Environmental Award from the College of Mount Saint Vincent in 2001.

and given John's stubbornness, he is not likely to be persuaded, but perhaps others can be. Armed with statistics and research, Horgan makes a case for an evolving society that will ultimately choose peace over war. Horgan is unapologetically optimistic about our species, reminding us that peace and conservation are mutually reinforcing behaviors. Given my knowledge of John's reverence for the human capacity to be altruistic (firefighters who risk their lives to save others is a common example that John uses), I imagine he may also be cautiously optimistic about our future.

In 2000, New York Governor George E. Pataki appointed John Cronin to help develop "a global center for river and estuary research." Pataki announced in April 2003 that the City of Beacon, New York would be the home of the Beacon Institute for Rivers and Estuaries[4] and that the 64-acre Denning's Point, a state-owned property near an ecologically significant area in the Hudson River, would be the future site of the Beacon Institute's campus. John was first named interim chief of the Beacon Institute and the board of trustees appointed him director and CEO in 2006. Jim Heron, retiring from forty years as an Episcopal priest, was soul searching for his next role, when he met John in 2003. There was an instant mutual appreciation and Heron found his place at Beacon Institute volunteering as a storyteller, speaker, and teacher about Denning's Point.[5] Through his research about the Beacon Institute site, Heron and John both saw how "the future possibility is illuminated and supported by knowledge of the past of Denning's Point."

John's new chapter of leading the Beacon Institute has nicely paralleled his own evolution of thought on environmental activism and partnerships. This message is clearly conveyed in Anthony DePalma's piece as he describes his 2005 *New York Times* interview of John in his new role. Although I've heard the statement many times, I am now wondering if that interview was perhaps the first articulation of the Cronin phrase, "The 20th

[4] Then called The Rivers and Estuaries Center on the Hudson. Its name changed to the Beacon Institute for Rivers and Estuaries in 2006.

[5] Based on his research, Jim Heron authored *Denning's Point: A Hudson River History* (New York: Black Dome Press, 2006).

century was the era of environmental brawn, the 21st century must be the era of environmental brains." Based on John's belief that "there isn't room for permanent enemies anymore," DePalma expands on this notion that "big corporations, once considered adversaries, now are potential partners because they possess the technical know-how and the dollar to get things done right, especially when government is dragging its feet." Throughout the essay, DePalma makes observations about changing paradigms (some changes are better than others): collaboration v. confrontation; conservation v. regulation; corporate partners v. adversaries; greenwashing v. genuine stewardship. Ultimately, he concludes that solutions to environmental problems are complex and they require a pragmatic new environmentalism.

As John was transitioning from the Hudson Riverkeeper to CEO of the Beacon Institute, his position at Pace University segued from an active role at the Pace Law Environmental Litigation Clinic to Resident Scholar in Environmental Studies within the Dyson College of Arts and Sciences (2000) as well as director of the Pace Academy for the Environment (2002). During this time, John was able to continue his love of teaching while pursuing his ever-expanding range of interests to include civic engagement, writing, literature, history, and policy. While contemplating the Pace Academy's mission, John began conceptualizing an ecosystem-based higher education collaboration. Immediately after graduating from Pace Law School, I was fortunate to launch the Pace Academy alongside John, and together we brought his vision into reality by jointly founding the Environmental Consortium of Hudson Valley Colleges & Universities (2004). Through the consortium of over fifty institutions[6], we have brought together faculty and students of diverse disciplines from a range of institutions across the region. With interdisciplinarity as the Consortium's guiding principle, faculty who likely would not have otherwise met are now collaborating and learning from each other.

Among the beneficiaries of the Consortium programming is Susan Fox Rogers who found that she and John have overlapping pedagogical, scholarly, and life interests in writing about the

---

[6] There were fifty-one institutions when this book went to press.

Hudson River. A self-proclaimed "outdoor woman," Rogers has edited eleven anthologies, primarily about outdoor adventures of women—from the Antarctic to the wilds of Alaska. Currently at work on her latest book, a collection of personal essays about the Hudson River from the perspective of her kayak, Rogers surely has much to teach John and vice versa. In her essay, she describes an at-times harrowing paddle down the middle of the Hudson, dwarfed by tugs and barges. Her reflections along the way reveal a side of John that few people perceive— his generosity with sharing knowledge; deep moral sense of the world; contagious optimism and bountiful hope about the potential of the future. With John as her garrison, she ends her journey safely and realizes that *"learning a river is hard"* but worth every challenging moment.

An emerging sub-theme of this book is reiterated with a unique lens in Stephen J. Friedman's essay about environmental problem solving through innovation and cooperation. As a member of Beacon Institute's Board of Directors and as President of Pace University, Friedman is squarely situated within both of John's worlds. Friedman explains how John's focus on the Hudson River has incorporated the whole evolution of environmental regulation—from identification of threats to increased reliance on science application in a manner that has global applicability. Friedman postulates that a genuine collaboration between environmental protection groups, energy companies, and industry would represent a new stage in the environmental policy debate, giving rise to new approaches to environmental regulation. If policy-making is based on science and knowledge, as Friedman suggests it should be, his collaborative methodology would be a model for river and estuary management around the world. If John's vision is realized, the Beacon Institute will create such a model through its real-time monitoring / remote sensing research as well as the facilitation of a "circle of consultation" among science, technology, and policy making.

Under John's leadership, the Beacon Institute has adopted technological innovation as a central mission. Its River and Estuary Observatory Network (REON) will monitor the Hudson from "source to sea" through a network of sensors and robotics that provide real-time data to researchers, policy makers and educators. Among Beacon Institute's collaborating partners is IBM. Harry Kolar, IBM's Chief Architect for Sensor-Based Solutions, has written a user-friendly technical piece on how advances in technology allow for advanced understanding of our ecosystems. Kolar draws linkages between data-knowledge-wisdom and reminds us that "Data are the facts, the objective truths of the system devoid of context" and thus the necessary foundation of wisdom (with knowledge as the intermediary). Real-time monitoring sensors provide us with the facts through data collection, such as detection of increased nitrogen content. Knowing the instantaneous effects of increased nitrogen on the ecosystem might alert scientists and others who would act accordingly. Those who have heard John speak about this potential, know that his vision is to "hardwire the Hudson" so that students sitting at computers can watch schools of fish swim through the river and power plants will receive notification when significant fish populations are at risk of becoming victims of the cool water intake structures. Kolar tells us that data and knowledge are currently being generated by this new technology, but wisdom has not yet been attained—it is in the hands of environmental visionaries (like John) to apply the knowledge gained to foster policy and education.

In 2007, John met Mary G. Burns and learned about her solitary efforts to preserve a small island's archaeological treasures from looters. As Burns explains in her essay, this pivotal meeting provided unexpected exposure to the cause and put Magdalen (Goat) Island on the map, so to speak. Burns endeavors to educate the public (including looters) about the importance of saving archaeological sites on state land for future generations. She envisions a time when advanced technology will allow us to "look" into the earth to see layers of artifacts that inform the history of a site without the need for destructive excavation. During his first visit to Goat Island, John saw it as the "poster child for all the damage being done to archaeological sites, not only along the Hudson, but all over New York." Burns is hoping that with the resulting *New York Times* story, she will gain momentum toward new protective laws for archaeological sites generally and Goat Island in particular.

I remember the slight tension in the room about one minute after I introduced John Cronin to Alexandra Dunn at Pace Law School in the fall semester of 2007. Each steeped in water law and policy throughout their professional career, they immediately began debating the question, "Is the Clean Water Act a failure?" I'm not even sure how it came up—it was as though they had both been eagerly anticipating this moment for years. In her delightfully multifarious essay, Dunn discusses her position on the Clean Water Act successes and failures while also reflecting on her special personal connection to the river and other water bodies throughout her life. Dunn recalls, "Although I hadn't seen the [Hudson] river since 1977, something about being near it was as easy and comfortable as talking to an old friend after the passage of many years. The river felt like home. The river could ground and root us." It is no surprise that she and John have a deep regard for each other (Clean Water Act disagreement notwithstanding).

In a fitting final essay, Joseph Pastore, Jr., muses about John's unorthodox professional path. Pastore began to learn in depth about John's extraordinary route as he was researching and designing Pace University's first Center for Excellence. John helped Pastore and others reconstitute Pace Academy into the Pace Academy for Applied Environmental Studies and John currently serves as the Academy's Senior Fellow in Environmental Affairs. Pastore's essay examines the role of formal education—especially higher education—in human development. Among the issues contemplated is whether higher education is a fundamental human right and social imperative. Should there be a push for meritocracy versus aristocracy? Is formal college training essential to produce well-balanced, skilled individuals who can perform effectively and morally? (Certainly not.) Pastore proffers that John's professional life "may serve as a metaphor for the reform of higher education."

IV. Closing Thoughts

John Cronin's professional biography states that he has been "an advocate, lobbyist, legislative and congressional aide, commercial fisherman, author and filmmaker"—based on the essays herein, he should think about adding to this list: investigative reporter, innovator, educator, and humanitarian. I once told John that he reminds me of a chameleon—colorful, adaptive, changing, solitary, reclusive, requires hot climate...He looked stunned by the comment and didn't instantly recognize that it was well intentioned. I stand by the analogy, and frankly, find chameleons fascinating.

I can't help but wonder—what is next for John? What will he become in his future reinvention? How will he surprise us? Who will be involved in his next big idea? Of course, I don't know the answers, but I am excited about the prospect and hope to be part of it.

Michelle D. Land
Director, Pace University Academy for Applied Environmental Studies

KEEP ON:
A CONVERSATION WITH PETE SEEGER

Pete Seeger

"Keep On" is an edited transcript of an interview with Pete Seeger conducted by Susan Fox Rogers in spring 2009.

SFR: John began working on the river in 1973. He gives you credit for handing him a hammer and putting him to work on a dock in Beacon. Can you tell me what you were doing in 1973?

Seeger: I believe John showed up on the waterfront and I was busy trying to fix it up so we could use it as a platform for a little boat we had. There had once been a ferry dock there, ten years earlier. It could have been a wonderful recreation center. The Black people of Beacon all at that time lived on the waterfront. And probably somebody on city council said if you think you will get reelected by giving them a nice building, think again. So instead they sold the building for a small sum of money, not much, and nothing was there but the first floor. We did not buy the building. There was a diner near the ferry dock. And we had one friend in city hall and he said if you are looking for a place for your Clearwater group to meet, you can use the old diner. So for thirty-seven years now, I think it is, we've used the old diner free of charge, which belongs to the city. But the building was so rotten your foot went right through the floor, so we poured a cement floor and put in a stove, a couple stoves, and we've used it for a meeting place ever since. Now other people use it too; they have a farmer's market that uses it also. At any rate, I think it was rather cool weather in either the spring or the fall when this young fellow came and says, "Can I be of help?"

and I said, "You sure can." And I had a pickup truck, and the same man on the city council said, if you want some old lumber, we're tearing down a building over here, you can get some beams there. So we went up there and sawed away and got a batch of two-by-tens or three-by-tens from this old building and took them to the waterfront and started hammering them in place to be some kind of a safe place where people could get on and off small boats. I was talking optimistically—as I tend to—the river's going to start getting cleaner and it's going to be a lot of local organizations that do the job. Next thing I knew he was working with the Hudson River fishermen down in Garrison and calling himself the Riverkeeper. And he and his wife lived down in that little town of Manitou.

SFR: John often mentions your philosophy of it takes not one big effort to make a change but lots of little efforts.

Seeger: My philosophy ever since I dropped out of the communist party is what's going to save the world is not big things but many little things. Now there are several books on this subject I recommend to everybody, the book *Blessed Unrest* by Paul Hawken and the book *The Green Collar Economy* by Van Jones. They both are carrying out what good people for centuries have said from Thoreau on down that good things can be done even if you're not famous, do it right where you are. The great biologist René Dubos said "Think Globally, Act Locally." E.F. Schumacher quit a good job in England to come over here and say, "Small is Beautiful." And of course Margaret Mead, the anthropologist said, "Never doubt that a few committed individuals can save the world. In fact, it's the only thing that ever has." And the two books that I mentioned. Paul Hawken, a small businessman, he's half of Smith and Hawken Tools. Gardeners love them. But he's also an eco-nik and he spoke at a thousand places in the last fifteen years. Van Jones is a Black man from Oakland California and a very good speaker. He's now put into a book his basic thought. He says one solution can solve two problems. One is unemployment and the other is global warming.

I guess it's my philosophy that big things tend to get corrupted.

During the 1930s when I was a teenager the music America listened to came out of Hollywood or Broadway. And that's when I found out that there are a lot of people in little towns that are in a singing family that still sang old songs; they called them folk songs. And they were good, very good songs, whereas the songs from Hollywood and Broadway were often clever but phony. The exceptions prove the rule. One of these exceptions, two of the exceptions, were written by the same songwriter, at least the lyrics were. Yip Harburg—he wrote, "Brother, Can you Spare a Dime?" and "Over the Rainbow." And other people wrote the melodies and he chose good composers to write the melodies. When Harold Arlen first played him the melody, up and down the eighty-eight keys, Yip said, "Oh, Harold, that's for Nelson Eddy, not little Dorothy." Harold turned white. His collaborator turned down his great melody. They both knew Ira Gershwin, the brother of George, and at midnight they called him up saying, "Ira, we need your advice." He came over, listened to Harold play it, and said, "Harold, give it a little more rhythm and play it a little faster." They got the great song. And the producer of the movie wanted to cut it out. The two men went on a two-man-strike: "This movie is *not* going to be made unless this song is in it."

Powerful interests want to lull the people to sleep with their songs, not wake them up. I say that this goes in many fields. It's true. It would be nice to have five billion dollars passed by the State Legislature to put in an environmental university where the purpose of the university is to give out degrees for people in environmental science and environmental politics and environmental laws and environmental songs and environmental shoelaces. But you can be sure that the powers-that-be would co-opt and corrupt it.

I often quote Plato, though I don't know where he said it, that "it's very dangerous to allow the wrong kind of music in the Republic." I was also told there's an old Arab proverb "when the king puts the poet on his payroll he cuts off the tongue of the poet."

SFR: Plato didn't want music in the Republic, but he also did not want poetry. It's dangerous.

Seeger: He would allow it if it was the right kind.

SFR: But that right kind was very limited. So what it takes is someone to come along and build their own dock. . . ?

Seeger: I didn't know where John Cronin came from except he said he'd been working for an alternate newspaper and it went broke. He was looking around wondering what he'd do with himself. And I encouraged him to come see what's going on in the Hudson.

SFR: And that was it. You traveled a lot, around the world, and then settled here in the Hudson. There's lots of places that you could have gone. What was it about this area?

Seeger: My wife and I were really dead broke. We had two babies and were kind of sponging off my wife's mother who had three floors and a basement in Greenwich Village for one hundred dollars a month. And so she let us have a room for ourselves and our babies. But I was not raised in the city and at the early age of three I became very anti-city. I looked out of my parents' apartment at one o'clock in the morning because of a traffic jam that woke me and I said, "Cities are stupid." Why does anyone live in a city? Too crowded, too dirty, too noisy. Why don't people live in the country? My grandparents lived in the country about thirty miles east of Beacon in a small town called Patterson. They bought an old farm there. And I spent all of my vacations until about age twelve camping out in the barn with my father and my brothers. My parents split and I went to school in the country, first in Litchfield for five years and then near Hartford for five years. The schools I went to were surrounded by a lot of woods and I learned to use an axe and would be very happy living in the woods in 1949. By accident we discovered 17 acres at one hundred dollars an acre, if you can believe it, and we borrowed 1,700 dollars because we didn't have any ourselves. Three hundred dollars from the man I made records for and five hundred dollars, I think, from the man who contributed to some other cause. My mother gave me a hundred dollars and my father gave me a hundred dollars. We camped out until I finished building a cabin.

SFR: Well, lucky for the Hudson River.

Seeger: I'm now convinced that this "think globally, act locally" is a very important philosophy.

SFR: Your way of getting this idea out is that you speak and you sing. When you speak of the environmental college that will never be it makes me wonder how this idea can be taught. Doesn't it take something extra; I'm thinking of passion, love, empathy. I'm not sure that this can be taught.

Seeger: It's probably not impossible. Might be easier in a small college than in a big one. At this late age of 89, I think that in the future if there is a world still here, it may be cities that will save us. Because cities can teach the smaller towns the advantages of being diverse. There's a newspaper stand in Forest Hills, Queens, which sells newspapers in 182 languages. There's a tendency in a small town to say, "Isn't it nice to live here far away from *those* people?"

SFR: So what at this point is the thing we should focus on in this river valley? If we carry on your vision, what would that look like?

Seeger: Well they are full of contradictions, of course. You can blame the Clearwater for one of the biggest problems. We started cleaning up the river and the real estate business said, "We can make billions of dollars here." We filled up Long Island, we filled up New Jersey, now we'll fill up the Hudson Valley and we'll get rich, rich, rich. The Hudson Valley is doubling in population approximately every twenty years. This can't go on forever. I was arguing with a local politician and said, "We've got to slow down." He looked me in the eye, "Pete, if you don't grow, you die." At one o'clock in the morning I sat up in bed and thought, "If it's true that if you don't grow you die, doesn't it follow that the quicker we grow the sooner we die?" Unless maybe we can learn to grow in generosity, grow in common sense. Grow in the ability to talk with people we disagree with. That's one of the most important things we all gotta learn.

SFR: That's wonderful. What else do you see as environmental problems?

Seeger: The poisoning of the air, and the water and the soil is another. And of course oceans rising is a big problem. A very big problem and it's coming quicker than anyone thought. It rose more in the last twenty years than it rose in the last century. The scientists who measure these things think that it has risen a foot in the last century. But I'm willing to bet that it's risen a foot in the last twenty years. In Beacon we have extreme high tides come when there is a coincidental meeting of a lot of rain, a new moon or a full moon when you get unusually high tides and a strong south wind. And then all of a sudden instead of going up three feet every eleven and a half hours it goes up six or eight feet. The waterfront at Beacon every year has some high tides that come right in the sloop club. Cars go afloat in the Beacon parking lot. It floods once or twice a year, maybe more.

SFR: And that's one sign of global warming? So, there's still work to be done is what you are saying?

Seeger: Ooooh! I was fairly pessimistic after Hiroshima, I thought it would be only a few decades before somebody would drop one of those bombs and if we weren't killed we'd be poisoned by the fallout. But Eisenhower wouldn't let General Curtis LeMay start World War III. He tried his best; he was playing chicken with the Russians. In '62 during the Bay of Pigs he had a hundred planes in the air with messages to all the pilots saying, "Communication with Washington may be cut off. If it is, take your orders directly from me." General Curtis LeMay was in charge of what was called the Strategic Air Command. When

Kennedy's people found out he'd done that, they said, don't do that again. When he died in 1990 he was still grumbling, we would have been better off if we had had World War III in 1954.

The last story in my book—a revised, enlarged edition of a book I brought out fifteen years ago, which is a songbook and a memoir at the same time. Now it still has got the same title, "Where Have All the Flowers Gone?" but a new subtitle, a "Singalong Memoir."

This is the last story in my book. My father was over-enthusiastic most of his life. First about this, then about that, then about something else, then about something else. But at age 90 he said, "Peter, I can't convince scientists they have the most dangerous religious belief in the world. And the scientist I'm talking to says, 'Charlie, I don't have a religious belief. I base all my actions on observation, double-checked world-wide as all science should be and then draw logical conclusions.' Oh, no, I tell them, haven't you observed that there are power hungry people in the world, people like Hitler. They're all over. Is it logical to put in their hands the ability to destroy the human race? They protest, 'But you are attacking all science. If I didn't discover these things, someone else would.' And I tell them yes, if you didn't rape this woman somebody else would, so why not? They usually stagger away saying, 'You have no right to ask questions like this.' And I shout after them, face it, it's a religious belief. You believe that an *infinite increase* in *empirical information* is a good thing. Can you prove it? Of course they can not." My father turned to me with a wry smile and said, "Of course, Peter, if I'm right perhaps the committee that told Galileo to shut up was right."

SFR: There is someone who started a sort of revolution.

Seeger: I'm out to remind people there are different definitions of the word "revolution." The agricultural revolution took thousands of years. The industrial revolution took hundreds of years. The information revolution is only taking decades. If we use it and use the brains God gave us we just may be able to get some miracles accomplished within the next century. One happened last November [2008].

I have a grandson who was raised in Nicaragua. His Spanish singing and speaking is expert. I'm trying to persuade him that the next big change in the world could be uniting people of Latin America like never before. They don't have to be in each other's face every day but have some sort of a television program, which everyone in Latin America listens to. And they will find they are cooperating on projects. One week they'll say look what this man and wife are doing in Bolivia. Oh, look what is being done in Dutch Guiana. And they will suddenly find they are talking to each other like never before. Between the television and the Internet this can happen and one of the great results of this will be not letting Uncle Sam run their country anymore. Uncle Sam has controlled Latin American for 200 hundred years, almost, by giving money to the Army and Navy of the ruling class to keep their working people down.

Exceptions prove the rule. Costa Rica had a general who got elected president and he said, "We're wasting a lot of money on an army and navy. Let's put this money into education." And now Costa Rica has one of the best-educated populations anywhere.

SFR: So you have real faith in technology and the ability to bring people together.

Seeger: Well, it could save us if it doesn't wipe us out first. And, who would believe that T. Boone Pickens would come out in favor of wind power? Or that George Soros would spend his billions to educate people?

Getting back to John and the Hudson. Any big river or big lake could have a clean-up organization. A body of water big enough that people say, "Let's love it like it should be loved." A former Clearwater crewman found a man with a sixty-foot schooner and he only used it a few times a year, the summer and the winter, or something like that. He would rent it for a dollar a week to do a Clearwater job in the spring and the fall.

The new director of Clearwater is determined to get the young people of the five boroughs involved. It's slowly getting cleaner down there. And there are several organizations already at work. Have you ever heard of "Floating the Apple?" There's another similar group up in the Bronx called "Rocking the Boat."

SFR: What's your next project?

Seeger: My next project is trying to gracefully retire. Because the mail comes in literally by the bushel and the telephone rings every five minutes and my wife and I have got to simplify our lives. We're literally on the go twenty-four hours a day. We were woken up by the phone at 7:30 this morning.

Needless to say, I'm glad that John has stuck around the Hudson. He's probably been offered better jobs to go to St. Louis, or California or some place.

SFR: I don't think he could leave. This is his place.

Seeger: Tell John I send my best. Tell him to keep on.

SEARCHING FOR POLLUTERS IN THE SUMMER OF 1974

Jim Detjen

During the summer of 1974 both John Cronin (who I then knew as John Harris Cronin) and I were starting our careers. I was a new reporter for the *Poughkeepsie Journal*. John had just been hired to work for Clearwater, the environmental organization founded by Pete Seeger.

I wrote a story for the *Poughkeepsie Journal* about Tom Whyatt, who had been hired to work as the first part-time Riverkeeper of the Hudson River. Soon, I was introduced to John, at a time when he was running Clearwater's Pipewatch project, investigating violations of the federal Clean Water Act. I joined John in his canoe as he examined pipes that were discharging wastes into tributaries of the Hudson River.

We hit it off immediately. We were both young, idealistic, and without much money. We both had an irreverent sense of humor and a tendency to rebel against authority figures. We both loved getting outside on a warm, summer day and riding in a boat on a waterway in the majestic Hudson River Valley.

Some of my fondest memories are of going out on a story with John and Jim "Whitey" Deckner, a legally-blind, award-winning photographer for the *Poughkeepsie Journal*. (I'm not making this up. Whitey, who was an albino, was so near-sighted that he couldn't pass a driving test. But he had an unerring instinct to discern visual patterns and to shoot some remarkable photos.) We would venture out onto the Hudson River with commercial fishermen to help them catch striped bass or search for the source of oil oozing out onto a waterway, causing the surface to glisten with an iridescent sheen. What a great job it was to be paid to go out on an environmental adventure with John and Whitey! I'd then come back to the office to write a story about the experience for the Sunday environment page in the newspaper.

One day John told me about an obscure company known as Tuck Industries and said he had evidence that it was violating the federal Clean Water Act. We both paddled along the Fishkill Creek and John pointed out twenty-seven pipes from the company's ancient factory that were discharging a foul-smelling gunk into the creek, a tributary of the Hudson River. Whitey took photos and I scribbled notes on my reporter's pad.

As I recall, it wasn't easy convincing my editors at the *Poughkeepsie Journal* that we should publish the Pipewatch project's allegations that the company, which made adhesive tape, was violating federal pollution laws. This wasn't the kind of soft feature story that the paper usually published. What if we got sued for libel? But in the end, I was able to convince my editors that the company lacked the required permits and was illegally discharging wastes. The story was published.

John took his evidence to the U.S. Attorney's Office in Manhattan and convinced them to prosecute the case. The office charged the company with twenty-fourviolations of the federal water-pollution statues in June 1975. Ultimately, Tuck Industries admitted violating twelve counts of federal statutes and was fined $43,500.

This success emboldened John to pursue other violators of the Clean Water Act and launched him on a remarkable career as an environmental activist, organizer and educator. The story about Tuck Industries convinced me that you could successfully publish important articles, if you had the documents to prove that the allegations were true. It helped launch me on a career as an investigative environmental journalist

Now, thirty-five years later, the episode seems like a lifetime ago. Yet, it also seems somehow like it only happened yesterday.

Like many journalists, I moved onto larger newspapers in search of better opportunities, both financially and professionally. After working at the *Poughkeepsie Journal* from 1973 to 1977,

I left the paper to get a master's degree in journalism from Columbia University. I worked as the environmental writer for the *Courier-Journal* in Louisville, Kentucky from 1978 to 1982 and from 1982 to 1994 as a science and environmental reporter for the *Philadelphia Inquirer*. In 1990, I was one of the co-founders and the first president of the Society of Environmental Journalists, an organization that now has more than 1,500 members.

During my newspaper career, I wrote many stories that prompted state and federal investigations and helped clean up environmental pollution. I won many journalism awards and in 1994, I was offered and accepted a position known as the Knight Chair in Environmental Journalism at Michigan State University. In 1999, I founded the Knight Center for Environmental Journalism, which is now the leading center for the teaching of environmental reporting in the country.

Both John and I have followed our passions and have had successful careers. During the past thirty-five years, environmental concerns have moved from society's fringes into the mainstream. We've been able to maintain our youthful idealism while raising families. I believe we both have played an important role in educating the public about critical environmental issues.

People magazine once described John as "equal parts detective, scientist and public advocate." I would add to this description "investigative reporter." If John had gone to work for a newspaper, I have no doubt he would have climbed through the ranks to become a top investigative reporter at a major news organization. John has the intelligence, passion and self-confidence to believe in what he is doing and to push his way though brick walls to get documents that confirm his hunches.

Along the way, some people perceived John as cocky and even arrogant. "He is a brash young individual who is obsessed with his own importance," Ralph J. Kirkpatrick, a former supervisor of Newburgh, New York, told *People* magazine after the town was prosecuted in 1986 for dumping sludge into a Hudson River tributary based upon evidence collected by John.

I never saw John as arrogant. He was—and is—a passionate

environmental crusader. He believes strongly in what he is doing but also has the ability to laugh at himself. His lifetime of outstanding work is a testament that an individual really can make a difference. I'm grateful for the chance to have been able to work with John at the start of his remarkable career.

Rediscovering Water Stewardship's Legal Foundations

Nicholas A. Robinson

Water's abundance is its blessing and its curse. Water is essential to our ecosystems, to human health and well-being. Earth's abundance of water shapes our hereditary mental outlook toward H_2O. When it is readily available, we take it for granted. It will rain soon; the rivers keep flowing. When it floods, the Common Law treats water as a "common enemy," and we do battle with flood waters, calling out our National Guard to protect our homes and businesses and lives. When there is a drought, we build canals and reservoirs, build desalinization "plants," or dig deeper wells to siphon our groundwater, many left by the glaciers eons before. Fishermen know, first hand, how clean water is needed for the ecology that sustains the fish they seek. Hunters value wetlands for the habitat that they provide to migratory ducks and geese, and all other migratory birds. But no one government, in any nation, has synthesized its "water law" into a coherent statutory framework. Some countries, the United States included, have tried to manipulate rainfall, and seed the clouds, but no nation has sought to protect and sustain the hydrologic cycle itself, the water vapor and great engine of weather patterns. Any restatement or codification of the many dimensions of water law lies in the future, if there will ever be a time (or the time) systematically to rethink our water law regime.

Our human society's needs for water are the driving force for shaping water law. We have done so instrumentally, seeking to secure specific types of benefits from water resources, or to ameliorate problems such as our pollution of water. Few of our laws are based on what the advances in scientific knowledge tell us about aquatic systems of life. When Congress defined the goal of restoring the "biological and chemical integrity" of the nation's waters in the Federal Water Pollution Control Act Amendments of 1972, it had taken a moment to acknowledge that the then scientific diagnosis of the deteriorating health of surface waters reached a moment when law reform was needed. When the Cuyahoga River caught fire, the public did not need a fisherman or a scientist to issue the alarms.

The history of water law in the U.S. tells a story of how public values, norms, policies and laws evolved from treating water as a "given" or a commons of no particular value, to being regarded as an essential component of ecological systems and of human endeavors that humans needed to manage in order to sustain the benefits derived from waters. Even waters apparently "unused" by humans indirectly provided vast "ecosystem services" upon which the human society depends. An awareness even emerged that non-human, non-instrumental values inhered in waters and their natural cycles, and so the United Nations World Charter for Nature declared that "Nature shall be respected and its essential processes shall not be impaired."[1] The Earth Charter later declared its basic principle that humans should "respect and care for the community of life," and that this entails "affirming that with the right to own, manage, and use natural resources comes the duty to prevent environmental harm and to protect the rights of people."[2]

Social norms grow in a society, whether in a village or a nation or internationally, in gradual and incremental ways. When a social value achieves a sufficient consensus, the society's law-makers formalize the norm as a law. Common law judges do it in court cases, and legislators do it in statutes. In each case, the law builds upon the consensus by accretion, over time. The progressive development of water law over the past century

[1] U.N. General Assembly, 48th Plenary Meeting, "Resolution 37/7 (1982) [U.N. World Charter for Nature]," (A/RES/37/7), 28 October 1982, http://www.un.org/documents/ga/res/37/a37r007.htm (accessed May 22, 2009).
[2] The Earth Charter Initiative: Values and Principles for a Sustainable Future, http://www.earthcharterinaction.org/content/pages/Read-the-Charter.html (accessed May 22, 2009).

offers ample evidence of the shift in public policy and law from ignoring and devaluing water, to treating protection of water as a high priority. There have been many disagreements and even battles over "water rights" through the decades, but as the consensus consolidates, the broad patterns of water law become evident.

It is timely to review this progression in water law, because human society is again at a "tipping point" which will test societal values about water. The growth in human population has made new demands on water imperative. More than 450 million people in twenty-nine nations currently suffer from water shortages, and this number is growing. The melting of glaciers will remove a traditionally assumed source of mountain water in less than two decades from now. Sea level rise is shifting human settlements inland, and an era of new and great migrations of peoples has begun. With satellite remote sensing and a new generation of technological assessment tools, humans can evaluate the human impacts on Earth's water resources, and assess the options for new water management systems. The new pressures on the hydrologic cycle and surface waters will remake the next generation of water law. That this prediction is so can be seen by a retrospective survey of some of the past century's water law innovations. This survey will reveal also the legal foundations upon which this new dimension of water law will be built.

Between congressional enactment of the Rivers and Harbors Act of 1899 and the Refuse Act of 1890, and the Federal Power Act of 1920 and the Federal Water Pollution Control Act Amendments of 1972 (FWCPA), the U.S. redefined the relationship of people and water. When the Constitution was drafted, the only concern the founding fathers had was to ensure that navigation would be open for commerce, and no state or person would impede equal and open use of the waterways. As the economies of the states grew, they tapped the surface and ground waters for their needs, allocating water rights on a "first come first served" Appropriation Doctrine basis in the western states and on a "reasonable use" Riparian Rights Doctrine in eastern states. Dams and navigation channels were allocated on navigable waterways by the U.S. Army Corps of Engineers and other federal authorities, and a mandate to respect and promote "multiple uses" of the nation's waterways was pursued. As pollution increased, Congress chose to invoke the Constitution's commerce clause to enact a vast public works program to build municipal sewers and publicly owned sewage treatment works, and the nation's industrial dischargers were obliged to obtain a "national pollutant discharge elimination system permit." Strict federal rules to prevent and clean-up oil spills were enacted, and in 1990 Congress allowed the states to impose even stricter laws to protect their waters and wetlands from oil pollution. As public access to the foreshores and waterways became difficult, Congress enacted the Coastal Zone Management Act and states established planning systems to avoid conflicts over coastal land uses while ensuring public access. Individual states also reinvigorated the Public Trust Doctrine, preventing acts by governments and landowners that would extinguish public rights in access to, and use of, surface water.

Symbolic of this systemic change in how society treated surface waters was the enactment of wetlands legislation. Prior to 1970s, wetlands were "swamps" and it had been state and federal policy to encourage their "reclamation" into dry land by draining and filling the wetlands. From the colonial period until the period after the World War II, over fifty percent of the nation's wetlands had been filled and destroyed. As biologists and hydrologists explained the importance of wetlands, states such as Massachusetts and Connecticut began enacting inland and tidal wetlands acts to preserve their remaining freshwater and saltwater wetlands. New York's Tidal Wetlands Act declared a moratorium on all filling of estuarine and coastal wetlands, which the courts upheld. At the federal level, efforts to apply the 1899 "dredge and fill" laws governing navigable water to include wetlands proved unsuccessful, and in 1977 Congress amended the FWCPA, rebranding it the Clean Water Act, and enacting new provisions to regulate wetlands. Federal authorities came to embrace a policy known as "no net loss of wetlands," which allowed some destruction of wetlands for development only if an equal or larger expanse of wetlands was restored someplace else. The zone between the dry land and the open water had moved from a "worthless" place no one wanted to protect, much less preserve, to an invaluable ecological resource.

Another hallmark of the new relationship of people to their waters was the Congressional sanctioning of "citizen suits." Pioneered by Robert Boyle and the Hudson River Fishermen's Association, lawsuits to protect the Hudson River from polluters, using the enforcement provisions of the 1899 Rivers and Harbors Act, proved their worth. Robert Boyle, a journalist and fisherman, had adopted the concept of a Riverkeeper from English common law, and transplanted it across the Atlantic and adapted it to the New World. Boyle's acumen allowed him to strategically use the law to protect the river. Congress enacted Section 505 of the FWCPA, and such suits spread across the U.S. Citizen environmental organizations invoked their right to enforce the water quality standards that federal and state environmental protection agencies had established for the surface water. Such suits were commenced to protect wetlands as well, as when the Fishermen's Association complained under the 1899 Act causing U.S. Attorney, Whitney North Seymour, Jr., to sue the U.S. National Guard for filling a wetland at Camp Smith on the Hudson River. Federal District Court Judge Morris E. Lasker ordered the restoration of the wetlands, which thrives to this day. In 1985, The Pace University School of Law established the first legal education clinic devoted to a single client, the Hudson River Fishermen's Association and its Riverkeeper. Boyle and his team had hired John Cronin to become the Riverkeeper, at the time, and the Association was reshaped as the Hudson Riverkeeper. Pace Professors and law students were the legal arm of the Hudson River. Through the extraordinary insight of one of the Pace professors, Robert F. Kennedy, Jr., the Hudson Riverkeeper became the prototype for a national and now international movement. The Delaware Riverkeeper, with a Pace Law School alumna, Maya van Russum, as its first Riverkeeper, and a Pace LL.M. graduate, Prof. James May at Widener Law School as its lawyer and legal clinician, replicated the Hudson model. Kennedy and Cronin, along with others, built a national Riverkeeper Movement, for Bays and Sounds, Rivers and Lakes, and then expanded it to a Waterkeeper Alliance in many nations. John Cronin's work was taken up by Alex Matthieson as Hudson Riverkeeper, and he with the Pace Clinic continues to serve the river. Cronin and Kennedy co-authored *The Riverkeepers*,[3] describing the model and their personal engagement in the effort. Writing while Vice President, Al Gore praised the two, noting, "The Hudson has shown a remarkable resilience in bouncing back from the years of neglect, and citizens living in the watershed have found that in their efforts to restore the river they are improving their overall quality of life as well."[4]

However, this progression in the law has not been uniformly beneficial to the ecology of rivers and surface waters. The courts have often sided with economic interests, preferring to allow exploitation of waters and wetlands. The U.S. Supreme Court has set up barriers to limit citizen access to federal courts, ostensibly to prevent busy-body lawsuits. The Congress has failed to fund the implementation of the Clean Water Act, precluding enhancements contemplated in the Act for further protection of water quality. Many states have cut back on their efforts to build coastal zone programs, and the volume of run-off pollution from urban and suburban streets and storm drains and farms lands is growing. Pollution has not ended.

Where citizens seek to keep the environmental laws robust and are vigilant about their water places, and where government agencies are loyal to their statutory mandates, this environmental stewardship of rivers, streams, lake and estuaries uses the laws to good effect. There are many complementary (sometimes still competing) users of surface waters: fishermen, mariners and boaters, the canoeist or kayaker, the tug and barge traffic on the inland waterways, the municipal drinking water utility, the enterprise or authority discharging wastewater into surface waters, the high school ecology class studying aquatic biology, the swim club or beach park, the water turbine through small-

[3] John Cronin and Robert F. Kennedy, Jr., *The Riverkeepers: Two Activists Fight to Reclaim Our Environmental as a Basic Human Right* (New York: Simon & Schuster, 1999).

[4] Al Gore, foreword to *The Riverkeepers: Two Activists Fight to Reclaim Our Environmental as a Basic Human Right* (New York: Simon & Schuster, 1999). 12.

head hydro or kinetic wave power producing electricity, the water mill, the farm or pastures or plant nurseries, and hosts of other users. Public uses of the waters are protected when a specific constituency exists for them, and speaks up for them, and invokes the protection of relevant statutes. This approach has its limits. Too often there is no specific constituency for broad public values resident in our estuaries and wetlands, such as the hydrologic absorptive capacity of the vegetation and soils, or their roles as nurseries for migratory fish or habitat in the flyways for migratory birds, or their presence as a natural open space. Even when Congress enacts laws and charges government agencies to defend diffuse public values, the record of effective government protection often is insufficient to protect the natural resources.

Examples of the lack of protection of our waters abound. The nitrogen cascade has grown enormously, and there are dead zones where no aquatic life can exist at the mouths of our rivers. Conditions for life in great ecosystems of the Chesapeake Bay or Long Island Sound or the Sacramento River Delta deteriorate. In drought conditions, the Mississippi River consists only of discharged, treated sewage wastewater. Electrical generating power plants discharge mercury and other chemicals into the air, which combine with the water vapors and precipitate our lakes and rivers, contaminating the food chain and imperiling life. The laws do nothing to safeguard the hydrologic cycle, and acid rain continues to destroy the living conditions for fish in the lakes of the Adirondack Mountains and the northeastern states. Invasive species, such as the zebra mussel, colonize our waters and change the ecological conditions. Lists of species endangered with extinction grow longer. As populations increase in urban and suburban centers, the incremental and cumulative impact on the waters of the nations grows too. Old standards have been left in place, even while they grow obsolete.

The nation's laws governing the waters of the United States have not been comprehensively examined since 1972. Congress has enacted no significant new statutes nor amended existing laws since 1990. Human impacts on our waters have increased gradually every year. The standards and objectives of the Clean

Water Act, the Coastal Zone Management Act, the Endangered Species Act, and the National Environmental Policy Act with its requirements for environmental impact assessments, are essentially fifty years old. Other related laws are twice as old. None have kept up with changed conditions. The dereliction of duty, on the part of Congress and the President, to protect the environment and learn from scientific analysis during these years has left the aquatic natural systems of the U.S. to deteriorate in measurable and marked ways.

All other considerations being equal, the neglectful application of the environmental laws enacted to date underscores, need for federal and state governments to reconsider their programs to protect the aquatic ecosystems of the U.S. Congress needs to remember how to analyze complex problems and undertake conscientious law reforms. For example, in 1973, the National Water Commission released its report *Water Policies for the Future*.[5] The future has come and gone. Congress needs to request a study by the national Academy of Sciences about the challenges to the nation's waters, and needs to constitute a law reform commission to study how to reconstitute the nation's environmental laws to meet the contemporary challenges.

Several states have done so. In 1995, the states and Canadian provinces around the Great Lakes prepared a Great Lakes Compact agreement, and enacted in the ensuing years identical statues in each state and province for the stewardship of the waters and ecological systems of the Great Lakes. In 2008, Congress gave its approval to the Compact, and President Bush signed the approval into law. The framework now exists to create a contemporary system to assess the aquatic resources of the entire Great Lakes watershed. The Compact provides for an integration of the water stewardship laws of all the states and provinces, and binds the federal authorities to follow the state systems. A rolling system of cumulative impact analyses of human effects on the Great Lakes is required, with reports every five years. This insightful legislation needs to be replicated in

[5] National Water Commission, *Water Policies for the Future*, (Washington, D.C.: U.S. Gov't. Printing Office, June 1973).

other watersheds. For instance, the Hudson River Watershed is largely the responsibility of New York State, and the State legislature could easily enact the same process for the Hudson, or for other great watersheds in New York. New York and Vermont could do so for Lake Champlain. The obsolete compacts for the Colorado River, which have allowed an over-draft of more than all its waters, need to be replaced with the newer model.

However useful the Great Lakes initiative will prove, the current state of the law is inadequate for the challenges looming ahead of the nation and the Earth as a whole. The United Nations' Intergovernmental Panel on Climate Change has identified disruptions to the hydrologic cycle as among the most dangerous. These disruptions are one effect of alterations caused by the accumulation of greenhouse gases and the increases in temperatures. The Hadley Centre for Climate Change in the United Kingdom has modeled the changes that are underway in the hydrologic cycle. Drought and sustained drought is likely, with some extensive and intensive flooding in other areas. The two can happen at the same time, and in the same region, because floodwaters can do their damage and then run off quickly without recharging depleted ground waters.

Many changes in human behavior toward natural systems, waters and wetlands, will be needed if human wellbeing and the human economy are to become sustainable amidst climate disruption. For instance, an entirely new network of surface reservoir, of water supply systems, of deliberate replenishment of aquifers, and of related ecological conditions is needed. New measures to promote robust biological diversity will need to supplant the gradual deterioration trends. The "no net loss of wetlands" policy will need to be replaced with aggressive freshwater wetlands restoration programs for river swamps, basin swamps, cypress domes, gum swamps, shrub bogs and depression swamps. The estuarine and coastal wetlands will need to expand with more mangroves planted, and measures taken to assist the migration of saltwater wetlands in to upland areas in advance of and during sea level rise.

In the wake of climate disruption, extreme drought is predicted to spread in the southwestern United States; there will be human migration to the coastal areas and the northeast and the Great Lakes basin. Similar circumstances will be reshaping population centers in China, India, Africa, Eurasia, South America, and elsewhere. If the U.S. can quickly pioneer the new land use and water regimes needed to sustain the quality of human life and biological diversity, it can provide models and practices that can be replicated in other regions on Earth. Similarly, the U.S. might learn from innovations in other lands that are ahead of us: for instance, in the coastal adaptations and reservoir development in Singapore, or the coastal zone protections against sea level rise in The Netherlands. By enacting new building codes to require "green roofs" and retain or harvest rain waters, run-off pollution can be minimized and systems to recharge aquifers can be established. By aggressive afforestation programs, watersheds can be restored, waters retained in watersheds, and biological diversity can be maintained. If the nation takes climate change seriously, suburban sprawl will need to end, new agricultural practices and soil conservation measures will need to be developed, and energy efficiency measures must be maximized. Use of coal and fossil fuels will need to be replaced by renewable energy systems, and the demand for new nuclear power plants will make new demand on cooling waters.

Will all of the changes to waters and aquatic systems be addressed carefully, in a proactive planning process, as was once the case with coastal zone management? Will we create a new regime for "coastal morphology," or the reshaping of coastal natural and manmade infrastructure to accommodate the reality of sea level rise and the storm and erosion consequences? There are new scientific models that may be established in place of the static and obsolete systems now contained in the Clean Water Act. For instance, "Resilience Thinking" offers a new set of tools for sustaining ecosystems and the human dependencies on ecosystems services.[6,7] Local governments will need to learn how to absorb disturbances and maintain essential functions. Today, they are at risk, and when disruptions destroy local land uses,

[6] Carl Folke, et al, "Regime Shifts, Resilience, and Biodiversity in Ecosystem Management," *Annual Rev. Ecol. Evol.* 33 (2004): 557-8.

[7] Brian Walker and David Salt, *Resilience Thinking: Sustaining Ecosystems and People in a Changing World*, Washington, D.C.: Island Press, 2006).

the waste and detritus washes into the waters, exacerbating the already existing degradation.

This retrospective of water law and policy from the late 19th century to the early 21st century brings to mind Yogi Berra's concept of "déjà vu all over again." The U.S., like all other nations, is at the brink of a radical era of new law-making to adapt to new conditions. The anthropologist Brian Fagan has described how civilizations in the past have coped with such fundamental shifts in climate. He states:

> Now, with warming accelerating, the stakes for humanity are much higher. Today, we harvest water on an industrial scale—from rainfall, from rivers and lakes, and from rapidly shrinking water tables. Many of us [in California] live off looted supplies, brought by aqueduct from the Owens watershed, culled from the Colorado River, taken from artesian wells, aquifers that will one day run dry...Today we are experiencing sustained warming of a kind unknown since the Ice Age...By 2030, UNESCO also estimates, the world will need 55% more food, which translates into a growing demand for irrigation, which already claims 70% of all freshwater consumed by humans.[8]

Perhaps the last word can come from Al Gore, in his foreword to *The Riverkeepers*: "In a profound sense, our rivers are a part of our national commons—a meeting ground where Americans from all walks of life gather to trade, reflect, rejoice, and restore. As we moved into the twenty-first century with a renewed sense of stewardship and appreciation for our rivers, we must carry that spirit with us."[9] The time is past due for an environmental amendment to the Constitution of the United States, to reflect society's current consensus about our stewardship duties

[8] Brian Fagen, *The Great Warming: Climate Change and the Rise and Fall of Civilizations*, (New York: Bloomsbury Press, 2008), 238-239.

[9] Al Gore, foreword to *The Riverkeepers*, 12-13.

toward water and all ecosystems; having a constitution that addresses water only through the 18th century's "navigation clause" is beyond being anachronistic. It is unjust. The coming climate change battles over water allocation and quality will be the crucible in which we "cook" this new amendment to our nation's most basic law. Most other nations have amended their constitution by adding an environmental provision. The U.S. is woefully behind in taking this basic step to consolidate its own consensus over water stewardship.

Renewing human environmental laws governing our care of rivers and estuaries will allow our communities to refresh and renew their kinship with the ecological systems of which humans are a part. Law reforms will emerge in watersheds, along rivers, around lakes, next to estuaries. As part of nature, human lives are shaped dynamically by the natural forces of climate change, just as we humans have induced the climate change. As we shape natural and human systems alike to adapt to the effects of climate change, we shall invent a new body of environmental law. If the past century of environmental legislating is a guide, then the tools of citizen engagement, as in the organizations of civic associations and their suits, and the respect for nature embodied in wetlands preservation and restoration, will serve us well as the coming century unfolds.

AN ENVIRONMENTAL CHAMPION FOR NEW YORK: MAURICE HINCHEY

Paul Bray with Congressman Maurice Hinchey

The modern environmental movement took shape in the 1960's and 1970's as a result of a series of key events in New York State and around the nation. On November 2, 1965, the people of New York voted 4-to-1 for a $1 billion bond issue for clean water. Shortly thereafter, a federal court recognized the rights of the Scenic Hudson Preservation Conference to challenge, on environmental grounds, the proposed Storm King pump-storage facility on the Hudson River, which is now regarded as the birth of environmental law. In 1972, New York State codified its environmental conservation laws. Congress also acted. It passed the Clean Air Act in 1970 and the Clean Water Act in 1972. With these actions, the seeds were planted for broadly protecting natural resources, the environment and public health.

The period between 1979 and 1992 was an extraordinary time in meeting environmental challenges, developing tools for protecting environmental quality and public health, and charting a course for the future. One of the major figures of this era was Maurice Hinchey, who served as the Chairman of the New York State Assembly Environmental Conservation Committee during this period.

Now a senior member of the U.S. House of Representatives, Maurice Hinchey served eighteen years in the New York State Assembly beginning in 1975. During his tenure, Hinchey distinguished himself as New York's environmental leader, initiating and leading a remarkable number of groundbreaking actions to protect and clean up the environment. His initiatives ranged from addressing environmental problems like hazardous and toxic contamination to fostering traditional conservation efforts and advancing a new and innovative form of parkland— the heritage area and greenway that encompass whole urban areas and landscapes.

In the 1970s the nation, including New York State, had to confront the huge challenge of cleaning up and regulating the great amount of hazardous and toxic substances that came from unregulated American industry.

One of Hinchey's first challenges as Chairman of the Assembly's Environmental Conservation Committee was Love Canal, the nation's first discovered major toxic dumpsite. After receiving reports of the situation at Love Canal, Hinchey's committee conducted a thorough and successful investigation into its causes, which Hinchey considers "one of the most appalling environmental tragedies in American history." The committee held hearings at Love Canal and took testimony from local homeowners and families. Hinchey and the other committee members were personally moved by the human suffering of people who lived in homes built over contaminated sites. Hinchey and Assembly Speaker Stanley Fink brought a copy of the findings from the Love Canal investigation to Congress and helped expose the nation to the tragedy. As a result of Hinchey's investigation and the public outcry it generated, further actions to address the critical issues of the region—especially dealing with the needs of families where homes were contaminated by the toxic materials around and under them—were then addressed by the state and federal governments.

Following the Love Canal investigation, Hinchey delved deeply into the history and impact of hazardous and toxic pollutants. He recognized early on that the story behind pollution "involves many villains, but a considerable amount of the environmental damage that has been done to our planet is simply a result of ignorant, under-regulated or careless industrial activity."

John Cronin worked effectively with Hinchey at this time on a variety of important environmental issues. At times, Cronin would even sleep on the couch in Hinchey's Assembly office.

After learning about hazardous substances being found

in municipal landfills, Hinchey led another high profile investigation; this time, into organized crime's control of the waste-hauling industry. The investigation resulted in the conviction of twenty criminal figures, including one for murder, and its findings were contained in a 1986 report "Organized Crime's Involvement in the Waste Hauling Industry," [1] written by the Assembly Environmental Conservation Committee. After that report, Hinchey believed the new environmental laws alone were not adequate to end organized crime's role in the waste-hauling industry and he continued to be a vocal advocate for tough enforcement of environmental law.

The results of these investigations, and others that Hinchey led, generated enormous public pressure for action and helped focus attention in the New York State legislature and in Congress on the need to develop programs to identify, investigate and clean up inactive hazardous waste disposal sites, as well as regulate ongoing treatment, transportation and disposal of solid and hazardous waste.

With hundreds of inactive hazardous waste sites throughout the state posing a threat to public health and the environment, New York was often the national leader in developing landmark environmental legislation. With leadership from Hinchey, New York's Superfund law was enacted in 1979 which, like the Federal Comprehensive Environmental Response, Compensation and Liability Law ("CERCLA"), established a basic statutory framework for identifying, investigating and remediating inactive hazardous waste disposal sites.

New York's regulation of the transportation of hazardous and non-hazardous waste was a forerunner to the "cradle-to-grave" tracking system which now exists at the state and federal level. With regard to solid waste management, New York was also in the vanguard of establishing the hierarchy of reuse, recycling and recovery of a wide variety of waste materials.

The rapid industrial growth in the 20th century created

[1] Assembly Environmental Conservation Committee, *Organized Crime in the Waste Hauling Industry*, report prepared by Chairman Maurice D. Hinchey, July 24, 1986, available from Assemblyman Maurice Hinchey, Room 625, Legislative Office Building, Albany, NY 12248; phone (518) 455-4436.

enormous challenges to New York's world class natural resources like the Adirondack Park, Catskill Mountains, and the Hudson River. Hinchey faced those challenges head-on by helping to secure the nation's only constitutionally protected wild forest land, developing the nation's first law to control acid rain through sulfur standards, and becoming the leading voice and driving force behind the call for the cleanup of PCBs dumped in the Hudson River by the General Electric Corporation.

An environmental legislator could have easily just been consumed with the Love Canal, PCB and acid rain-like issues in the 1970s and 1980s, and not done much else. For Hinchey, it was only the beginning. He created a broad, diverse and deep legacy relating to protecting and improving natural and cultural environmental quality.

Early in Hinchey's legislative career, he was an advocate for local and healthy food long before the current trend. Hinchey chaired a Food, Farm and Nutrition Task Force that advocated for the family farm, local food and food safety at a time when industrial agriculture had predominated.

Hinchey also helped ensure that one of the great American landscapes and sources of history, the Hudson River Valley, was preserved and protected through cooperative planning and management. New York's Hudson River Valley has been called "the landscape that defined America" with scenic beauty captured by the Hudson River School of Art, rich natural resources and a heritage associated with dramatic and insightful stories of America. Unfortunately, as the 20th century unfolded, these treasures were at risk of being lost to history because of the balkanized systems of management that were in place. In order to address this pressing need, Hinchey led the enactment of innovative heritage and greenway legislation that has been a unifying force of many units of government and, in effect, between man and nature.

Among the fruits of Hinchey's efforts in New York State are the Hudson River Valley Greenway, a management program for the Hudson River estuarine district and its fishery, and more than twenty state heritage areas, including five in the Hudson River Valley. The Hudson River Valley Greenway is the most ambitious greenway initiative in the nation, encompassing a portion of New York City and total land areas of counties on both sides of the Hudson River from Westchester and Rockland counties to Saratoga and Washington counties at the northern end.

The greenway law provides an innovative "compact" approach with incentives to regional planning, authorizes the creation of a Hudson River Valley Greenway Trail with portions on both sides of the river and establishes an intergovernmental Communities Council to create and coordinate public actions and foster planning within the entire greenway.[2] The genius in Hinchey's greenway structure is establishing the means and purposes for intergovernmental and public-private collaboration strong enough to attract traditional anti-regional, pro "home rule" local governments to actively participate in the planning and activities of the entire greenway and heritage areas.

The Hudson River Estuarine Program that Hinchey's legislation created has grown from a river fishery oriented program to a comprehensive action agenda program with goals that include protecting river scenery, waterfront revitalization, pollution reduction and promoting water quality for swimming in the river. This program has been identified by the Ocean and Great Lakes Ecosystem Conservation Council as a model for basin programs throughout the state.

In 1982, the New York State Legislature enacted landmark Hinchey legislation to establish a statewide system of heritage areas. Like the greenway, heritage areas are an expansion of the notion of state and national parks from being public estates or features (owned by the government) to encompassing entire landscapes and urban settings. Heritage areas are a form of park made up of mostly privately owned land. They are managed through activities designed to achieve the intersecting goals of conservation, education, recreation and sustainable development. Hinchey included state funding for visitor centers in each of the original thirteen state heritage areas in the 1986 Environmental Quality Bond Act. This act by the state helped forge the partnership between the state and local governments

---

[2] New York State Hudson River Valley Greenway, http://www.hudsongreenway.state.ny.us/ (accessed May 25, 2009).

that is necessary to plan and manage living parks or heritage areas.

When Hinchey entered Congress in 1993, he immediately began working to replicate and support his work at the state level by authoring legislation to create the Hudson River Valley National Heritage Area. Through his tireless advocacy, Hinchey secured passage of his legislation as part of the Omnibus Parks and Public Lands Act of 1996 that was signed into law by President Bill Clinton on November 12, 1996. The Hudson River Valley National Heritage Area, along with several other heritage areas created in that act, were amongst the first of its kind and paved the way for other National Heritage Areas to be designated in the future. Today there are forty-nine National Heritage Areas across the country.

Fortunately, Hinchey's interest in improving resource management capacity did not end with rivers and estuaries. Hinchey was also a sponsor of the state's coastal zone management program.

Many of Hinchey's efforts fall under the category of being a visionary. Yet Hinchey also has the will and capacity to be a problem solver. For example, land acquired by the state in the Adirondack Park must be "forever wild." This policy was tested when the state purchased the Sagamore estate in the 1980s. At the time, the estate was made up of forestland, a lake, a lodge and related buildings. The small village area had a blacksmith shop, barn, schoolhouse and other buildings that supported the functioning of the Great Camp. The state ensured that the lodge would be preserved by having the facility purchased by a non-profit preservation organization. However, the state acquired the village buildings would be destroyed, which was inconsistent with the forever wild requirement. When it was brought to Hinchey's attention that the village area was integral to the historic "Great Camp Sagamore," he initiated a public discussion of the issue and developed a solution. It was a state constitutional amendment allowing the sale of the village property to the preservation organization. The amendment was approved by the voters. Now, Great Camp Sagamore, including the village with its twenty-seven authentic buildings, is a National Historic Landmark dedicated to education, interpretation and historic preservation and is accessible to the public for tours and overnight programs.

In the Catskill Mountain watershed where the New York City reservoirs are located, conflicts emerged between New York City, local communities and fishermen when the city ignored local interests. As a problem solver, Hinchey negotiated and advanced a water release act, that for the first time required New York City to release from its reservoirs water to sustain the fishery of streams affected by the reservoirs.

Hinchey actively supported funding for sustainable wood product businesses in the Catskill Mountain region. Before leaving the New York State Legislature, Hinchey was able to enact legislation for a Catskill Park visitor center, which is still being developed and has recently picked up momentum through state and federal appropriations. Communities in the Hudson River Valley Greenway counties, which were originally excluded from the greenway because they were also within Catskill Park boundaries, have petitioned and received authorization to become part of the greenway.

Another of New York's great natural resources, Lake George, was also the focus of Hinchey's environmental protection efforts. Lake George in New York State is renowned for its scenic beauty and water. The lake's watershed provides unparalleled residential, economic, recreational, and environmental opportunities. In 1791, Thomas Jefferson wrote, "Lake George is without comparison the most beautiful water I ever saw. Its water is limpid as crystal and the mountainsides are covered with rich groves of fir, pine, aspen, and birch down to the waters [sic] edge."[3]

When issues of deteriorating water quality due to increased development and invasive species were brought to Hinchey's attention in the 1980's, he spearheaded the enactment of basin legislation that authorized storm water, wastewater, and stream protection laws that would apply throughout the Lake George Basin.

Another success occurred during the early part of Hinchey's

[3] Lake George Association, http://www.lakegeorgeassociation.org (accessed June 3, 2009).

career in Congress when he initiated and led the successful effort to preserve Sterling Forest, the last significant area of open space in the New York metropolitan region and an important watershed for southeastern New York and northern New Jersey. The protection of more than 20,000 acres of Sterling Forest stands as one of the greatest examples of cooperation between various public and private entities in recent history.

The bipartisan, two-state initiative to purchase the lands now constituting the Sterling Forest State Park was an enormously complex undertaking, involving many partners, including the federal government, the states of New York and New Jersey, and a host of private foundations and organizations. The result of the long and laborious process to save Sterling Forest was the creation of the largest public park system in the New York metropolitan region since World War II. This safeguarded land will benefit future generations through the protection of drinking water supplies for millions of individuals, the preservation of critical wildlife habitat, the conservation of the region's biological diversity and the enhancement of the recreational and scenic resources that serve one of the most densely populated regions in the country.

CREATING THE FOUNDATION FOR THE FUTURE

Many of Hinchey's state legislative achievements on hazardous, solid waste and toxic regulation and the creation of the Hudson River Valley Greenway and the state heritage area system are enduring legacies, but Hinchey was also concerned during his New York State Legislature years that the means should be available to advance the environmental agenda into the future.

Use of conservation easements and ongoing funding from the Environmental Protection Fund have been major driving forces to advance the state's environmental agenda since Hinchey left the New York State Legislature. He was the sponsor and major advocate for codification of conservation easement legislation, allowing non-profit organizations to use easements to protect scenic and historic areas, open space, and other cultural resources. The conservation easement law is considered to be a landmark environmental law. The Environmental Protection Fund, with dedicated revenue from the real estate transfer tax, provides the life blood for much the state's environmental program.

Common law easements do not run with the transfer of land and therefore are not binding on subsequent owners unless benefiting contiguous property owned by the holder of the easement. Hinchey's legislation specifically provides that conservation easements limiting development or use of real property for conservation purposes are enforceable whether or not it is appurtenant to the holder's (whether they are a public body or non-profit organization) interest in real property.

The conservation easement law opened the door to a flourishing land trust movement protecting open space including farmland across New York State. In the case of the Adirondack Park, for example, hundreds of thousands of acres of private forest land has been protected as open space for future generations by conservation easements.

The 1993 Environmental Protection Act is the other major foundation builder in Hinchey's state environmental legacy. This act was sponsored and strongly advocated for by Hinchey following a failed 1990 environmental bond act. The 1993 Act created an ongoing fund with dedicated revenue to support land acquisition, landfill closure, municipal waste reduction or recycling projects, park, recreation and historic preservation projects, local waterfront revitalization and coastal rehabilitation projects amongst other environmental objectives that have grown over the years. The 2009-10 State budget appropriated $225 million for these fund projects.

CONCLUSION

Maurice Hinchey's commitment to public health and environmental quality and his legislative skills while a member of the New York State Legislature are unsurpassed and will endure as a legacy benefiting future generations. After leaving the State Legislature, Hinchey's achievements have productively continued to the present time in the U.S. Congress, but this is another chapter.

Duty Bound:
A Conversation with Henry Gourdine

Henry Gourdine

"Duty Bound" is taken from a recently found recorded interview conducted with Henry by John Cronin in the summer of 1982.

One More Year

If it was necessary, I'd go and ask the boss for the time. And if it was necessary to quit, I quit. I'm not lying to you. It's true. If they like me good enough to invite me to come back again, or tell me that there was a chance at the job again, alright. And then I would make every effort to go back. If they didn't, they said, "Well, if you go, you're gone." Thank you, been nice knowing you, and walk. Without never a look back.

I was able to look out of the back of the shop window, and I looked down the river, and I saw the guys out lifting their nets. Well now, see, I would get the fever. So I would go to the boss, and I'd ask him. I'd say, "Now, they're catching a lot of fish down the river, and they're making a lot of money. Now, could you let me go a little bit sooner?" And he said, "No, our agreement was such-and-such." Well, I'd be so mad I could spit in my own eye.

I was only getting, at the time, maybe $25, $30 a week, because that was the pay then. It was in the '20s. It was pretty good money. But I would convince myself that those guys was doing good. So, I'd come down around the river, and I'll bet you the first week that I was there—I wasn't fishing, or anything, I was just trying to get the rig ready—I don't think those guys ever made not $30 in a week. I don't think they were making $6 a week. But I was there. I was free. I was happy. And there was no such thing as unemployment. You were strictly on your own. But that was before I was married, too. Even after I was married I did it all my life.

For the second year we were married, I promised my wife that

I would quit fishing, because she didn't like the fishing. But she had kind of gotten used to it, because I was fishing when I was going with her, and she knew I always seemed to have a jingle of change in my pocket. Fifty years ago, a couple years after I was married, I promised her I'd quit. And she said, "One more year." And I'd fish one more year. We did that right up until the time she died, and still fishing. So, I never was able to keep my word. That's one thing that sometimes makes me feel a little bad, that I broke my promise to her. But then again, if that's the only promise I ever broke, I guess it's not too much to worry about.

If I had a carpenter's job, or whatever, at the time—"Sorry, but I'm gonna have to be leaving in two weeks." Meanwhile, I always was a gentleman. I'd give you two weeks notice. "What's the matter?" "Nothing. I'm just going fishing." Some of them would understand, some of them would get into it, and be serious, and ask me what time I would be through, and how long it lasts, and all that stuff. Would I be willing to come back? And if I like the job good enough, I'd say, "Yes," and I'd be willing to come back. And if I disliked it enough, I would say, "Well, Lord knows when the job is going to go—when this fishing is gonna finish." I said, "I might fish all through the season." That's when I didn't want the job anyway. I never missed a season.

Came to the River Riding

And then there was one time, there, two years, didn't do anything else but fish. I fished the river in the spring for shad. And then, just as soon as that was over, it was getting time to go to the lake, the reservoirs. And I worked for people that had permits to take the carp. Go up to the lake, every morning, go carp fishing. I been in all of them. Any of them that would support a net, I been in them—and always the outboard motor, which is strictly against the law. But our boss gone to the same club as the Commissioner of Water, Electricity, and Gas, in New York City. And we were instructed to use that motor, wherever we went. Anybody said anything, say nothing but just keep on going, all around Kensico Reservoir. And that's a no-no, over there. That can put you in jail, quicker than anything. But we did it.

That would go into the summer. Now, pretty soon, let's say by the 15th of August, we're going to start cutting the grass around the beaches, so a net can come in free, for the haul seine. First of September, we start the haul seine—put it in late summer or early fall, bass fishing. By the time that was over, then it was time to go on the outside, fall fishing. And we did that. And we fished until pretty near time that we were going to get ice. We were scared of the ice coming. So we tried to pull the nets out, pull the poles out, pull the boats out. And then, the old ice would start to melt. And then we'd watch, every day, to see if these different holes closing up—up in the bay, that big expanse of water—maybe half as big as this dock. We'd have a severe cold night, next night. And all that closed up. And then we'd try the ice, keep trying it. Finally, we decided it's thick enough. Go up and put nets under the ice.

So we'd fish on that as long as the ice lasted. Sometimes we'd have to put the nets in, two or three times, because we'd lose them. And then it's getting along towards spring. We'd have to start thinking about getting some stuff ready for the spring shad fishing. So that was right around the corner. There was some time left in between, but we figured we had earned that rest. So we never worried too much. But it became less lucrative. So we did away with some, continued others. We left off the lake fishing. And we tried a little summer fishing, for carp. And the price went so low we got disgusted, and we give that up.

Some years, one year I can tell you in particular, it was either 1928 or '29, We could not catch fish. It was one of those stinko seasons. Where we ordinarily fished 1,200 feet of net in the river, we run an extra set of poles in on the shoal water and we put an extra 400 feet. Well, after expenses was paid, once a week, we paid a man. And things were so bad that one week my partner said, "Well, you take the money this week. You take the profit. I'll take it next." Come the end of the season, we barely had money enough to pay the management. I had an old Cadillac car—sold the Cadillac car, put the money in the business. Came to the river, riding. I walked home. I didn't have a dime in my pocket. We owed a $40 grocery bill.

A Day's Work

And I had other seasons where you might say I just broke even. But I always tried to see that my family had enough. And I also tried to see if there was an extra dollar, that it didn't need to be spent, to try to keep that, because I know that there's always going to be some lean days coming. And that's how we got along. And then my wife, she was a very conservative sort of a woman, she used to do a lot of canning, stuff like that. And that kept us going.

Anyplace that I worked, as a rule, I was always lucky enough to be welcomed back again. I don't say that I was the best carpenter in the country. I know I wasn't but I always tried to give a man a day's work. So I worked with unions. And they would say, "Well, we've made money enough for the boss, this morning. Let's take it easy, this afternoon." I didn't work with them very long. I'd find an excuse to get away from them. I never figured that was right. I figured if no matter how good you did—say, for instance, you were getting $25 a day and, in the morning, you had made that $25—I say that's no reason to pull your punches and take it easy. Because if you can make him another twenty-five, or fifty, in the afternoon, do that. Because some days, even though you're working for yourself, you can try as you will, and you will not produce. And you're very anxious, because it's you.

On the other hand, it's equally hard—there's just going to be days that you're not going to be productive for your boss. So if he hasn't something made up, something built up, some reserve built up, how's he going to offset that? Because that's a complete loss; you haven't even made your wages. And I knew it was necessary to operate that way, if you expected your boss to stay in business. Now I never went and kissed no boss's ass. But I figured I owed him that. And I could give it.

The Fire

I must say I have no regrets. It ain't always been that lucrative. Because I spent considerable time and money, trying to build up an outfit. I went from an outfit where we put together two rows of net—one row of 1,200 feet, and the other one, 800 feet. That was in 1934. And my partner decided he didn't want to bother no more. So I bought him out. And the winter before I had taken a power boat over to Croton Point and ripped it all to hell on the rocks. Took the old engine out. Took the false floor out, inside. Put a new bottom onto it. Cut the sides down, about four inches. Put new chines, new skeg, new shaft rod, to run the shaft through. Put the boat right side up, and raised the sides. Put a new rib alongside each old rib, raised the sides, eight inches. I put in a new towing post, a new bit in the front, one in the back, new decks, new deck timbers, brand new engine.

My boat slip ran way back in, big enough, maybe for a 150-foot steamboat to lay in. Of course, it's all sand now. But that was 30 feet of water. So I would always operate that way—I tried to keep the powerboat that I had already fixed, kept it over there. It was a big lumberyard, great big lumberyard. So there was a game, down at the prison. And two busloads of people came from the city, going down that Main Street hill. And they were supposed to turn in, going to the prison —that wall, going down to the junkyard that led to the prison, and it still does. And the guy, one of the fellows, lost his brakes coming down that hill. And he kept bumping against the walls, to try and slow himself down. When he got to the station ramp, he couldn't make no turn. He got to the station ramp, he come up the ramp, and, instead of making the turn, he come down this way. Plunge right across, into the lumberyard. And then the bus exploded, quite a fire. A lot of people got burned. Some got killed. And set that lumberyard on fire.

My wife came down to the river, and she asked a couple of guys, "Would you go over, and take that boat out." She realized that boat was going to get it. So they went over there and, like damn fools, they tried to start the boat. She says, "See! You don't start it! You just cut the line, untie them, whatever, give the boat a push out in the river." They went back again—so hot, they couldn't get near the place. The boat burned, right there. No insurance, or nothing. And then it was all on me, because I had bought the business.

And I had a whaleboat, a big navy lifeboat. We bought it from some guys who were going to make a powerboat out of it. And we used to hire this other whaleboat from this guy, for five dollars. We used to bring this up, put it with our boat, put the cross pieces across, and that was the pole boat. That's what we carried our big channel poles with, towed them. And that boat burned. So that left us with our whaleboat. I say "us." It left me with my whaleboat, because I owned the outfit.

Too Dumb Lookin' to Be Crooked

This is 1934, the beginning of 1935. I had to start the shad season. I had no boat to carry the poles. I had a pair of scows. These scows were two-inch plank, twenty-four feet long, four feet wide, thirty inch deep, which today would cost you a fortune, made out of fir. Then, that took the place of the whaleboats. Then I realized I needed rowboats. Built two of the nicest round-bottomed boats you ever laid your eyes on—half-inch cedar planking, white cedar, oak ribs every eight inches, eight inches from center, and planked over with this white cedar. Oak stern, oak bow, oak keel, mulberry floor timbers, one of those every eight inches, same as the ribs. And the ribs were all along sides, and butted on the keel. They were natural bends. I climbed seventy-five percent of all the trees around this part of the country, to get those. And they were taken and ripped out. Then, there were four knees for each seat. Four knees. There was three seats in the boat. That meant twelve knees. There was a natural breasthook. And it had two natural ribbed knees on the corners of the stern. They come out on the stern, and they went alongside the gunwales. All copper riveted.

And the boats were made a little bit different. The second boat, that was going to be mine, I broadened the stern out a little bit. Made it a little more flat. They didn't have a vertical deadrise. They didn't come up quick like that. They come up gradual. I want to tell you, they were beautiful boats. And they could carry the weight. So I had to build them. I didn't have nothing else. And on top of that, I had to build another motorboat.

And my father helped me with the boats. Helped me with the

scows. And I went down to New York; I went to Brooklyn, to see this man, an old man. He owned that place, the lumber company. They had the cedar logs laying out in the creek. So when they needed to saw some up, haul 'em up, cut 'em up into lumber. Hell of a place. I went to see him. My father explained the situation to him. And asked him if he could just get this lumber ripped for me. So he says, "Why are you in such a hurry?" So I explained to him. I said, "I lost my boat in a fire. And I just bought the business and I bought my partner out. Lost his boat to the fire. And I gotta be ready." He says, "Oh. We'll do our best."

We had an agreement, now you listen to this, Twelve cents a foot for the best of white cedar, not no bullshit. Once in a while you find a knot, a very small knot. And the theory is that if it doesn't come out when they're planing, when they're dressing the wood, then it won't come out. But I never used to take no chances. If it was a small knot, I'd get a cork, and I'd put it in there. And he said, "Wow, you've had tough luck. Instead of charging you twelve cents. I'm going to give you this lumber for eleven cents." I'd never saw the man before in my life. So I said, "Sir, I don't have money enough to pay you for all this lumber, at this juncture." I said, "I've got just so much money, $300. Will you, when you get this lumber ready, send this amount of lumber for the amount of money that I'm going to leave for you." And I said, "In a week or so, I will be ready to take the other. Could you operate that way?" "Oh yes," he said. So I paid him the money.

After a fair balance of time, I thought there's something wrong. I said, "Tomorrow, I'm going to call that man." By Jesus, that very afternoon, when I was contemplating calling him, the next day a truck pulled up to the place, my father's place, and he wanted to know where I wanted the lumber. So I told him it had to be down at the dock. And he said, "I can't get this big truck down there. I'll have to unload it up here. Have to carry it." I'm looking and it seems like a hell of a lot of lumber. Not more than I ordered, but more than I expected. I come to find out the old man had sent the whole order. And he sent a little note of explanation. He said, "You go right ahead with your project. And when you get the money, then you can pay me the balance."

Never saw the man before, and he never saw me. The only way I could figure out why it ever happened that way, I suppose the man looked at me and said, "That son of a bitch is too dumb lookin' to be crooked." So he let me have it. That's the only way I could figure it out.

THE RED DRESS

Our property, the second lot, ran down to the river. And there used to be an old scow down there. They used to work on the bridge there. And I'd go into the house and my mother would say, "Don't you go down to that river today." So I'd gradually work my way down the end of the lot, which overlooked the river. And I'd see the kids all down there, some would be swimming, some of them would be fishing. So I let it be known that I was up there.

"Come on down."

"Nah," I said, "I don't feel too good."

"Ah, you'll do all right. We're getting a lot of fish. So-and-so got so many crabs. Somebody's got a rock bass, somebody's got some sun fish. Young perch."

"I haven't got any fishing pole."

"Use mine."

I had a fishing pole. The fishing pole was right in the bushes. I was trying to be a good fellow. You know, do like I promised my mother, I wouldn't go into the river.

"I can't."

He said, "Why?"

I said, "I ain't got no bait."

"We've got plenty."

Everything to help me get to the river. So I looked back toward the house. I didn't see nobody. Down to the river. Didn't realize how time was passing. So, soon I looked up, and at the beginning of the path I see my mother standing there. She was down at the foot of the hill, right near the path that I had to take to go up there. So I gave the kid back his fishing pole.

"Don't you want the fish?"

"No, you keep 'em," I said.

So I get a full head of steam, and I start. Had to go past my mother. She used to have an arm full of these cherry shoots, you know? Maybe about six feet long. And boy, she started on me going up that hill. And she could run just as fast as I could and faster, too, I guess. The only time she'd ever have to step out of the way, I'd be knocking these big sand stones loose and she'd have to step out of the way to keep them from hitting her. And she'd wail on me all the way up to the house. But when I got up to the house, she'd finished. She raised hell.

So I'd stay around the yard, and play there, and by 1:00, why, I was sufficiently cooled off to make the trip again. Down I'd go again. And in less time than ever, she'd be standing there in the path, when I went back later. And I'd get it again. But it just shows you how stupid some kids are. That didn't mean nothing to me. Next morning I'd do the same thing over again, the next afternoon, same thing. Twice a day for the summer, I got it.

To keep me from going down to that river she sewed me a red dress and made me wear it. One time she started to get ashamed of herself. In fact, she said she did get ashamed, and that's why she took the dress away. She said, "Because it was so badly torn." I used to climb trees and everything. She said, "There was a piece of that dress on practically all the big trees in the neighborhood."

I'd climb the trees and tear a piece of it. I used to keep right on going. It didn't bother me. It was long, too. I used to pick the dress up when I was running. Run, just like these ladies when they've got the long skirts on, when they want to go upstairs or something.

I wore the dress, all right. And I don't know how long it took me. Things that a kid will do. I was just naturally born crazy, I guess. I'll tell you the truth. If I had it all to do over again, I don't regret any of the time. I would start right over again, I would still be a fisherman.

DUTY BOUND

Charlie Rohr's father was the first man I went fishing for. When I was a little kid, I used to go down to the river and watch him mend the nets. I sat down on a log near him. When he said, "Well, I've got to go up to the shanty and get a drink," he would leave his needle, and I'd grab that needle and mend the nets. I'd mend, and I'd make mistakes. I knew when I had made a mistake. I didn't know how I'd made it, but I knew that I had made a mistake. Put that needle right back in that net again. And sit on the log. Look.

Finally he'd come down, pick up the needle. Right away, he'd see there's a mistake. Curse himself backwards and forwards for being that stupid, to make a mistake like that. And he'd explain to me, he'd say, "Now, you see?" He said, "I should have taken up back there, instead of that. Now, I've gotta cut that out." So, I said, "Well, don't do *that* no more." And I didn't either. But when it come time for me to go with him, I could mend as good as he could. And mend it right, too. I was only the second man that I ever knew that he would allow to put a needle in his nets, he was that fussy. He didn't like no crooked meshes, or anything. He wanted everything right. And he wasn't a fast mender, because he cut the cords and the fingers on one hand, and he never could straighten his fingers. I could outdo him after a while, when I got to be good at it.

Tucker Crawford always says, "You know, Henry," he says, "It's too bad that someone in your family hasn't taken it up too"—like building a boat, and rigging the nets and fishing the nets, and understand the different types of gear. And he says, "It's a sad occasion. First, to accumulate the knowledge that you have over the years, and then you're not able to pass it on anywhere."

That's one of those things. And perhaps if people were interested, or if anyone was interested, it wouldn't be so much knowledge that I could pass on to them, but I could get them started in the right way so that if they were at all interested, they would be able to pick up some of that knowledge themselves. I'm a funny kind of guy. I was so much dedicated to the fishing, when I see somebody else that seems to be trying to learn the business, trying to pick up what they can about the fishing, then I feel I'm almost duty bound to try to help them.

DAVID AND GOLIATH:
FOR THE LONG HAUL

Robert F. Kennedy Jr.

I met John Cronin in mid-February of 1984. I liked him instantly. Six foot, two inches, with piercing blue eyes, he was eloquent, thoughtful and utterly committed. John was fearless in the face of big government and big business. He understood the impact of the legislative process and knew how to mobilize the region's best attorneys and scientists. He knew every commercial fisherman and most of the anglers, biologists and conservationists on the Hudson River. He believed strongly that a safe environment was a democratic right and was indignant when government agencies didn't take seriously the sacred obligation to protect the Public Trust.

I was impressed by John's honesty, his courage, his humor. He always lined up with the underdog. His approach to the river was guided by his experience with families and communities that depended on the Hudson for their recreation, their livelihoods and their property values during his days as a commercial fisherman. His was a kind of blue collar environmentalism that appealed to me. John was militant in his defense of democratic governance, the integrity of the public trust and human dignity. He saw human beings as part of the landscape he sought to protect, and he saw the Hudson as a community—where sports fishermen, commercial fishermen, river pilots, oil tankers, barges and pleasure boats might enjoy the bounties of Creation and support their livelihoods.

John had a great sense of humor and an extraordinary talent for politics. He thought about tactics and strategy in a way I admired. Robert Boyle (journalist, outdoorsman, and founder of the Riverkeeper organization) had just appointed him

Riverkeeper and gave him a meager salary and a $15,000 annual budget. John was living in his Toyota pickup which also served as his office. Then John Adams persuaded the State of New York to lease us the farmhouse at Castle Rock, the old Osborne estate, for one dollar a year. Despite the discomfort and inconvenience of his current circumstances, John only grudgingly settled in at Castle Rock. I remember his unease at changing his mailing address, certain that when the state officials administering the estate realized its new tenant's subversive mission they would find a way to terminate the lease.

When I began working with the Fishermen (Hudson River Fishermen's Association), our approach was kamikaze. John had almost no cash flow and yet he was delivering legal broadsides to the biggest corporations and most powerful institutions in America—Con Edison, the U.S. Army, New York City, the Federal Department of Transportation, Exxon Oil and New York State. Early on he explained his guerilla philosophy. He told me that if he had only a few thousand dollars and came upon a polluter he would attack even if it looked like the effort might jeopardize the organization. This apparently self-destructive strategy made sense at second glance when one considered that his opponents could always outspend the organization. The Fishermen relied on stronger spirit, conviction, idealism and tenacity to prevail. The organization's purpose, John often reminded me, was to protect the river, not to build an institution.

For John, the Riverkeeper was a law enforcement organization. We had great environmental laws on the books, but they were mainly ineffectual due to the political clout that enabled polluters to capture the regulatory agencies and derail serious enforcement. Without enforcement, the public was not getting the advantage of the wonderful environmental laws that federal and state legislatures had passed to protect their citizens. John pointed out that law enforcement doesn't just punish violators: it moves the moral milestones of a culture. Even in the Hudson Valley where enforcement was generally more aggressive than anywhere else in New York State, most polluters had little or nothing to fear. We saw first hand how institutional cultures within the environmental agencies encouraged routine acquiescence to pollution and to a gradual decline in environmental quality. Hopelessly out of touch, the New York State Department of Environmental Protection (NYSDEC) and federal Environmental Protection Agency seemed hardly to know that the Hudson existed or that their lax enforcement was putting fishermen out of business, devaluing property and destroying communities.

In the early 70s, John had worked as a liaison between the Hudson's commercial fishermen and NYSDEC. At that time the agency was assembling the list of fishes it intended to ban due to contamination by the very PCBs that it had earlier permitted General Electric to dump into the river. During a late night phone conversation with John, NYSDEC Commissioner Ogden Reid read down the list—carp, striped bass, sturgeon, white perch, yellow perch. He never mentioned eel, an important commercial fish in the Hudson. John was surprised, since the eel were among the most contaminated species. "Commissioner," he asked, "what about eel?" There was a long silence. Finally, Reid, caught off guard by the query, replied in exasperation, "John, we have not yet made the determination as to whether eels are fishes or snakes." Containing his outrage, John said, "With all due respect, Commissioner, that determination has already been made."

He never told the river men about Reid's statement. "They were already too demoralized. They felt forgotten by government and this would have just made it worse."

Despite an orgy of violations, there was little, if any, law enforcement. Corporate polluters like Con Ed and other utilities were illegally killing fish by the millions. Smaller dischargers rarely received enforcement attention. For example, both federal and state agencies, as a matter of official policy, would not even inspect polluters whose discharges were less than one million gallons a day and would not enforce against developers who filled wetlands less than twelve acres. An accumulation of these small dischargers, dumpers and bank disturbers could destroy an entire tributary without attracting any enforcement attention. In Bob Boyle's words, the Hudson was dying "the death of a thousand cuts."

Perhaps the most encouraging lesson I learned from John was that when government abdicated its law enforcement responsibilities, citizens could step into the vacuum and take the law into their own hands to protect a public resource. In our first investigation together, John and I, and Patrick Gilligan and Joe Augustine donned waders and spent weeks walking riverbanks, climbing fences, crawling up pipes and taking samples and we sat all night on lawn chairs waiting for midnight dumpers. We assembled evidence to successfully prosecute twenty polluters on Quassaic Creek, a troubled tributary in Newburgh, New York.

We gathered one-liter sample jars filled with red dye and sewage and alum sludge from textile houses and treatment plants. We photographed bulldozed wetlands, stacks of cinder blocks and piles of carts littering the creek bed. Altogether we nabbed twenty-four polluters including Mobil Oil and the Town of Newburgh and some of the most powerful financial and political interests in the Hudson Valley. I went to the law books and found a way to sue each of them. I learned from John that common sense and honesty, a willingness to read the law, and a strong sense of entitlement to a clean environment are the only necessary qualities for a good environmental advocate or lawyer. This is the approach that had worked for John in the Exxon case. When he caught Exxon stealing Hudson River water, he assumed that the theft must be illegal even though no law specifically prohibited it. He reasoned New Yorkers had not spent millions of dollars to clean up the Hudson to benefit Exxon. John had only his powerful indignation, his strategic skills and his sense of bravado when he went up against the biggest corporation on Earth. He brought the action under a range of statutes, utilized publicity, got the legislature and federal agencies involved, and finally forced Exxon to back down. Using the same approach on Quassaic Creek, we forced its polluters to rehabilitate a Hudson River tributary where lawlessness has become the norm.

John recognized that environment is not something distant and inaccessible to most Americans. The environment is our neighborhood, our community. It is the infrastructure upon which we construct quality lives. The battle for a clean environment is not just about protecting distant wilderness areas like Montana and Wyoming. It is intertwined with the battle for justice and democratic ideals and against the disparities in wealth and opportunity, problems of race and civil rights.

Newburgh's quality of life was certainly affected by the way it cared for its environment. Rather than celebrating its proximity to the Hudson River and Quassaic Creek, Newburgh allowed its shorelines and tributaries to become dumps and sewers, spoiling their value for its own citizens and the rest of us. Newburgh's morale followed its shoreline. Its lack of care for its environment was reflected in the disheveled and hopeless character of the city itself. Just as the restoration of Baltimore's waterfront led the way to that city's revitalization and moral rejuvenation, the destruction of Newburgh's waterfront clearly paralleled its moral and physical bankruptcy.

I began, in Newburgh, to see the environment not as a privilege that was part of my affluent background, but as a right for every American, one that was being subverted by greedy, powerful, selfish and corrupt interests within our society. When we first presented our evidence in the Quassaic Creek cases to the regulatory agencies, John and I told them that our goal was to return to every Newburgh child his or her right to go down to the creek with a fishing pole and pull out a fish for dinner. We might have added "or turn over a rock and catch a pet frog or salamander or swim in the swimming holes without danger of being poisoned". These are entitlements that no one has a right to subvert.

I feel responsible for the best and most important decision in John's life. In 1984, my friend Connie Hough had left her job at Kraft Foods after the company had been taken over by Phillip Morris, which removed the no-smoking signs, placed ashtrays at every desk and encouraged its staff to take up a new habit that would kill one of every five of its consumers who used its tobacco products as directed. Alarmed that Kraft's once-wholesome corporate culture had turned sinister, Connie was looking for a new job and I invited her to apply to work at the Pace Clinic. She was vivacious, friendly, brilliant, and well-organized enough to impose order on the wild chaos of our clinic's operations. With

Connie around, every day became a holiday and every holiday became a three-ringed costumed celebration. In 1990, John and Connie were married. I am so happy for the role I was able to play in bringing these two wonderful people together.

John recognized the corrosive impact of excessive corporate power that poisons both our democracy and the environment. He used to say, "There are never any permanent victories. The only thing that will save us and this river is permanent vigilance." Today the growing power of the river's polluters and the growing dysfunction of government make that vigilance more urgent than ever.

John's courage and perseverance gave us many victories and the organization he created has continued his legacy of David and Goliath victories even after he moved on. We've also had many defeats, but John taught me that sometimes you have to be willing to die with your boots on. I recall a meeting when someone passed around an article about a famous environmental lawyer who, after arguing the Storm King and other landmark decisions, had started his own boutique environmental firm and had begun representing corporate polluters. *The New York Times* piece had him saying, "The days of fighting big corporations is over. Now is the time for working together and finding common cause." John showed me the line and whispered, "If you ever hear me saying something like this, I'm begging you, please shoot me!" So I guess we'll have John around for the long haul swinging his fists against excessive and undemocratic corporate and government power in the eternal brawl to save the planet.

RESTLESSNESS

Alec Wilkinson

Possibly not everyone knows that John studied dance in college, at the University of Hartford. He thinks the inspiration to do so might have come from having as a child watched films of his parents in a minstrel show. He took a modern dance class in the fall, and a seminar over the winter break in New York with the Martha Graham Dance Company, and when he returned to college he auditioned for, and received, a scholarship to the Hartford Ballet School. For the rest of the winter, and some of the spring, when he might have been sitting in a classroom, he was in a studio with mirrors on the walls. His dancing career ended when he was riding one day in the backseat of a convertible, with his head laid back, staring up into a wide open blue sky, and, in the grip of "a moment of clarity," he says, he realized it was time to quit school and travel around the country; to wander in the wilderness, in other words.

To raise money for the trip, he took a job in the Catskills leading trail rides. He knew nothing about horses and was surprised at how big they were. The following February, he and his girlfriend left New York, with three other people, three cats and a dog in a Plymouth Valiant, for Phoenix, where they assumed it would be warm. They arrived in Santa Fe in a blizzard. Driving over the mountains, the car's temperature gauge fell so dramatically that John wondered if it was possible that the engine could freeze while he was driving the car. For the rest of the winter, he washed dishes in a Howard Johnson's and when the weather turned warm, he and his girlfriend drove to Boulder, Colorado, where they lived in their car. A collision in a parking lot damaged the car's radiator sufficiently that the car couldn't be driven. The man who owned the junkyard where the car was to be towed agreed to let them sleep in the car in his junkyard, but when they arrived there that night the car was still on the tow hook, so they found a Volkswagen bus that had no roof, then they found a door to stretch across the seats as a bed and some plastic for a blanket. During the day John sacked groceries, which he disliked. With a recruiter, he signed up to become a door-to-door salesman for a book company. The company sent him to a five-day sales school in Nashville. As part of the curriculum, the school invented a prospect called Mrs. Jones. Her husband was at work, her children were at school, and to engage her a salesman was not to ring her door bell but to knock on the door, a gesture that was regarded as being more personal; furthermore the novelty was likely to make her curious. When she opened the door, the salesman was to be standing with his back to her, apparently absorbed by the view from her doorstep, so that she would have to say something first. What John was to sell her was an edition of an enormous book called *The Volume Library*. To carry himself from place to place he had a bicycle.

His territory was in South Bend, Indiana, the home of Notre Dame University, where practically all the streets are named after Knute Rockne. He had the aptitude to sell books and the charm but not the interest and he gave up and moved back to Boulder, where he discovered that the man he had sublet his apartment to had persuaded the landlord to write a new lease with his own name on it.

Before long, John moved back east and worked successively as a carpenter, a roofer, a roofing salesman, and a bouncer. Then he volunteered for the Clearwater. The original Riverkeeper, a man named Tom Whyatt, who had a canoe, invited him to participate in a project called Clearwater Pipewatch, for which John took samples of discharges issuing from companies along the riverbank. Several companies were indicted from the results and an official at one of them described John as "a Boy Scout with binoculars." For a couple of years after that, John worked as a lobbyist for the river and for environmental causes and then by making the acquaintance of a master crabber and shad fisherman named Bob Gabrielson, in Nyack, he began working on the river itself. For two years he divided his time between lobbying and fishing, then in 1981, he gave up his apartment and moved into his truck, which he parked on Gabrielson's dock. Eventually he became a fisherman on his own. Driving down the river to retrieve his nets on the first night that he fished by himself, it was borne in on him that what he was looking for was a half-inch line in a three-mile-wide river.

From fishing he became the Riverkeeper, where he was able to apply almost everything he had learned since he quit ballet school, and before long he had managed one of the river's most spectacular environmental cases—the taking of Hudson River water to Aruba for use in refineries belonging to Exxon and the flushing in the river of the holds of tankers the company owned.

Not long after he had brought Exxon to court, I read about him in a newspaper and called to ask if I might try writing about him, too. Tepidly, he invited me to come to Garrison to the farmhouse where the Hudson River Fisherman's Association (HRFA), and the Riverkeeper, had its headquarters. I drove up from New York and when I got there, John wasn't there. The Fisherman's Association's new lawyer, Bobby Kennedy, was. He said John had left abruptly for White Plains, to buy a tie or something, I can't remember any longer. Bobby took me to a swimming pool about a quarter mile from the farmhouse to see if I could breathe underwater with an aqua-lung and then we went diving in a pond up in the hills, so I had a nice afternoon, but I didn't meet John.

Of the period we spent together, encompassing three seasons, I remember mostly how many trips I made to Garrison, waiting for John to say something revealing. I didn't take his reluctance personally, except maybe once, when I arrived expecting to spend the day with him, and he said he had forgot that he had a dentist appointment, but that I was welcome, so far as he was concerned, to sit in the waiting room, if I wanted. John would organize days in such a way that he wouldn't have to talk to me. He would take me to see Bob Gabrielson, or Robert Boyle, who can talk about the river for days, or invite me on to the boat with several other people to go fishing or when some local dignitary was aboard or when he was doing work, such as dragging for creatures for the

Museum of Natural History and needed to concentrate on the task. He was like an old Indian, who knows precisely the thing you want to learn but hasn't decided yet whether he regards your character as sufficiently trustworthy.

In those days John lived in a house on the river. He had bought it after seeing the *for sale* sign in the backyard, which the owner had placed so that it could be read from the water. Directly in back of the house, across a narrow gravel road, were the railroad tracks and past them a marsh—Manitou Marsh—made when the railroad had cut the land off from the water, and which was full of songbirds. John had a dog that liked to chase the trains. Trains arriving from the south would blow a whistle as they rounded a bend just south of John's house, and the dog would howl. When I rode the train to Garrison, I could see the house and sometimes John's car in the driveway and the dog racing like a rocket up the road. John's car in the driveway did not necessarily mean that he was home. He often came and went in the *Riverkeeper*, the boat the HRFA had made for him, and which he moored off the house. He once told me that one of the things he liked best about work was driving home in a boat. At night he could see the lights of the houses across the river, and all day and night the life of the river, the traffic and the ice floes and the things floating in it, like a pageant.

I put up with John's recalcitrance because I knew what he had accomplished and that someone who was frivolous could never have managed it. I could also see that by his nature he was a very restless person and likely didn't care for being described as being one way when he might have cast off that way of thinking or being by the time the description appeared. He was fierce in defending his sense of himself. I don't mean that he was oversensitive, I mean that he understood the value of and embodied the integrity involved in being an individual, of cultivating and refining one's thoughts and habits and beliefs, and sometimes discarding them completely and starting over again, and I regarded such an attribute as a sign of a serious person. I understand this twenty-five years later, but at the time I merely wondered why he was being such a pain in the ass. Eventually I wore him down. Or, even better, he might have concluded that I was someone with sufficient character of my own that I could be trusted to appreciate his.

His restlessness, I learned, was a habit from childhood, ingrained and stimulated by his mother and father, whom I never met. His father had been a middle level employee at Otis Elevator, in Yonkers, but had himself grown dissatisfied with his lot and had moved the family—John and a brother (later there was a sister)—to Baltimore. About his father and his influence John told me, "I have always had a feeling that I carry with me this idea of constantly moving to something better— even just something else." In Baltimore, John's father sold ice cream franchises, which had a predisposition to failure, and the family moved three times, making it difficult to make friends. In warm weather, John's father would show movies on the side of the house and serve popcorn and drinks and the kids would come and have a ball and the next day in school act as if they had never seen John or his brother, as if what had taken place the night before were a rite that no one spoke of. The family returned to Yonkers where John's father took up a lesser job at Otis, without his seniority. He had been a Time-Study man; someone whose job it is determine how long a task should take. Eventually he became a personnel manager. Otis was a factory from the early days of the century, with shadows and dust like a veil in the shop and numbing amounts of noise.

John's mother and father had the ambition to own a house, and weekends they would take the family to look at real estate they couldn't afford. The house they eventually bought did not have a bedroom for John. His father double-jobbed evenings, for a while at a shoe store. He also sold sporting goods and worked behind the counter of a deli. John would fall asleep in his parents' bed and when he woke in the morning he would be in a bed in the living room.

The other important idea in the family was the regard for work. John began working at Otis at fourteen, having lied about his age. His father expected his children to aspire to a college education, but his sons regarded him as a figure of authority in the hierarchy of the elevator company and seeing all that he had accomplished without a college education assumed that one was unnecessary.

When I was younger I always thought that my subjects had to be older than I was, in order to have something valuable to tell me. For years, John was the only person my age that I wrote about. I was aware that in the Exxon case, with the help of others, he had handled a challenging situation with distinction and aplomb. Fumbling it would have made him and anyone interested in the well-being of the river either a pest or a figure of ridicule. By winning the case, by arduously building it and skillfully managing it, he prevailed. He had absorbed an immense amount of information to make this so. He had also combined his gifts for clear thinking and resourcefulness with what he knew of the river itself, having studied it closely, like a scholar with a fascinating text.

I am not certain that I know anyone else who has conceived so many plans and brought so many of them into being. Sometimes years go by when I don't speak to John, and I am always surprised when I call and find out, not that he is doing something different from what he was doing last time I spoke to him, but that he has done two or three inventive and innovative things in the interval. His restlessness has moved him forward at a rate slightly higher than the rest of us, I think. There have been, so far as I know, no fallow periods. Only an immensely capacious and creative nature can build such a life requiring constant renewal and refreshment.

A Baykeeper's Story

Andrew Willner

Anyone who knows me also knows I love to tell a story. I want to tell a little part of the Baykeeper story—how it all began, gained momentum, and flourished, and how we wound up as the vital organization we are today.

I didn't grow up loving the Bays of New York Harbor. I had to learn how to care passionately for this scarred but unbeaten ecosystem. My first recollection of the Harbor, its waterways and wetlands, while growing up in northern New Jersey, was of smell and smoke. To get to New York City in the 1950s meant driving the Pulaski Skyway. Traveling that road, particularly at night, suggested Hieronymus Bosch images. Windowless factories spewed fire, smoke, and repulsive odors. The ride always evoked squeals of horror and delight from the back seat of my father's Oldsmobile as we entered the aroma zone of the Secaucus pig farms, and the burning garbage dumps.

My earliest activism came in high school when my friend David and I, wearing berets and with what little facial hair we could muster, attended SANE nuclear policy meetings at the Ethical Culture Society, mostly because we had heard that the "beatnik chicks" might be easy. Then in 1970, at the moment Nixon invaded Cambodia, and with TV images of dead college students at Kent State, my opposition to the war and my life in advocacy truly began. This soon led me to early efforts to save two living rivers: to help to stop the building of the Tocks Island Dam on the Delaware and the construction of nuclear power plants on the Susquehanna.

Much later, in the 1980s, after I had returned home to the Harbor, I worked as a wooden boat builder on Staten Island, just above the Narrows. Three experiences convinced me then that the battered bays of the Harbor needed a Keeper. My young daughter Emily came to play in the boatyard. On the hottest summer days I filled an old fiberglass dinghy full of tap water so she could splash and cool herself safely. It was both poignant and pitiful that we couldn't walk half a block to the beach, and swim in the Harbor. That the closest bit of sand was called "needle beach" was also a strong deterrent. The second experience happened when a huge fish, a prehistoric-looking sturgeon, lazily swam in and out of the boat basin. I watched its every move with wonder, just as at other times I watched herons hunt killifish in the shallows adjacent to the half-sunken wooden barges in the mud flats of the Arthur Kill. The third catalyst to my advocacy came when I started hearing about Riverkeepers on the Hudson and Delaware, a Long Island Soundkeeper, and a Baykeeper in San Francisco.

I was inspired by what was happening almost in my backyard. Bob Boyle (and his book, *The Hudson: A Natural and Unnatural History[1]*); John Cronin, the Hudson Riverkeeper; Pete Seeger and Clearwater; the Hudson River Fishermen's Association; Scenic Hudson; commercial and recreational fishermen, and thousands of community members who had joined forces to launch a grassroots revolution reclaimed the Hudson River as their own, despite its being used as an open sewer, and being abandoned by the state and federal governments. The miracle was that, thanks to these caring advocates, the Hudson was healing.

I pestered John Cronin and Terry Backer, the Long Island Soundkeeper, for months as I became determined to duplicate their work in the Bays of New York Harbor. In August of 1989, with encouragement and contributions from Riverkeeper and the American Littoral Society, Baykeeper was born.

Our baptism was in oil. On New Years Day, 1990, Exxon spilled 500,000 gallons into the Arthur Kill, a tidal strait separating New Jersey and Staten Island. I called Dery Bennett, Director of Special Projects (at the time Executive Director) of the Littoral Society and asked him, "What do we do when something like this happens?" He responded, "I don't have a clue, go figure it out." So I made it up as I went along. I went to the only

---

[1] Robert H. Boyle, *The Hudson: A Natural and Unnatural History*, (New York: W.W. Norton & Company), 1969.

accessible waterfront on the Arthur Kill. I literally moved TV news cameras toward me, and began to speak. To my surprise the reporters listened.

When Exxon claimed that the Arthur Kill was a lifeless waterway that couldn't be harmed by the oil spill, friends and I gathered up dead, oil-soaked birds in an attempt to force the company to tell the truth. When an Exxon guard asked me by whose authority I was ordering him to open the refinery gate to admit a pickup truck loaded with oiled casualties, I whipped out my only identification, a Hop-Along-Cassidy badge, and said, "Because I am the Baykeeper!" I told him if he didn't let me in, I would dump the dead birds in the lobby of the *New York Times*. After consulting with his boss, the guard let us in to the bird rehabilitation center where the victims could be added to the total killed. Later, I did get my interview with the *Times*.

During the Exxon spill I learned on the job about how oil doesn't get cleaned up, despite what the Coast Guard says; that birds and fish are affected years after a spill; and that oil kills salt marshes, despite their tenacity. I also learned how to sit through interminable meetings, to understand the insults to the environment hidden in bureaucratic jargon. And I learned how to take advantage of my place at the table. I also discovered that reporters and agency personnel, like everyone else, become advocates if you can just get them out on the water. I made the boat a tool as well as a symbol. I learned to be a loving guide, to show people beauty beyond the tragedy, and to make the Arthur Kill a symbol for positive change throughout the Bay.

I learned quickly that I did not know much, and that others with years of experience were willing to teach me. And I also found that assertiveness, bordering on aggressiveness, can serve the cause as long as it is tempered with information both accurate and consistent. The baptism of Baykeeper, in the oil of the Arthur Kill Spill, was a great first lesson in the sobering reality of urban environmental advocacy.

During the early 1990's, my passion for my Bays, my home, became both professional and deeply personal. The Harbor, I learned, is a productive ecosystem, boasting hundreds of species of plants, fish and other wildlife—and that a lucky wanderer can still explore quiet sandy beaches, fresh and salt-water marshes, rocky points, broad bays, and narrow straits. There are very few places like our estuary, where a fisherman could have a day like I had during a summer now ten years ago—a home run: a striped bass, a huge summer flounder, a weakfish, and a bluefish, all caught in Raritan Bay (on the same tackle and within a half mile).

One of Baykeeper's strengths has always been "wiseassiness," and I think that is a great description. Baykeeper has always been a first responder. When everyone else is running away from the toughest issues, we're running toward them, licking our chops and rubbing our hands. Over the years, that has meant that we've worked hard to prevent:

- the loss of our last urban open spaces to development;
- the loss of wetlands in the Meadowlands, Jamaica Bay, Raritan Bay, and the Kills;
- the failure of government to press for Natural Resource Damages from our worst corporate polluters;
- stormwater pollution and the disgrace of combined sewer overflows;
- nitrogen pollution from New York City;
- dioxin pollution on the Passaic; and PCB pollution in the Harbor.

Hardcore advocacy has always been the defining feature of Baykeeper's work. We love a good fight, even if some take decades to resolve. We especially enjoy a brawl in which the odds are stacked against the people and the environment, in which bad guy developers and polluters smugly assume victory because of their bloated wallets and backdoor political influence.

I'd like to focus on just two of those David and Goliath fights: one on the Hackensack in which we, along with a remarkable coalition, achieved a major triumph, and the other on the Passaic and in Newark Bay, which is ongoing.

There's little question that one of Baykeeper's greatest victories and environmental legacies to date is on the Hackensack River in the Meadowlands. From the start, we drew a line in the marsh that we would not allow developers to cross. We said that not one acre of wetlands would be filled in, and we stood by that declaration for more than a decade. We galvanized the public by showing again and again how foolish these proposals to fill some of the region's last wetlands really were. Ultimately, 10,000-plus advocates preserved over 8,000 acres of wetlands within five miles of New York City, and put citizens back in the driver's seat to manage those precious natural resources through the Meadowlands Conservation Trust.

Baykeeper is still fighting another decades-long campaign on the Passaic River against Occidental Chemical—one of the region's and the globe's most heinous polluters. A single Newark factory stands out for its deadly products and pollution, and for its shameful history on the Passaic. Diamond Alkali manufactured DDT and Agent Orange, and for years they dumped a deadly dioxin cocktail into the waterway. Because of these reckless practices, both the factory and Passaic River were declared federal Superfund sites. But as of today, almost 25 years later, the United States Environmental Protection Agency (USEPA) has done nothing to force Occidental Chemical (the successor to Diamond's businesses and liability) to clean up the river and Newark Bay.

Their dioxin has concentrated in the region's fish and crabs. It is also concentrating in the fat, breast milk, and reproductive organs of fishermen, their families, and those who just happen to live along the Passaic. The dioxin mimics hormones, breaks chromosomes, and raises havoc in our bodies. Despite more than fifteen years of advocacy in which Baykeeper clearly documented Occidental as the villain with the largest liability on the Passaic, the polluter concocted its own absurd proposal for clean up. Remarkably, this bogus initiative puts two of the most compromised federal agencies, the USEPA and US Army Corps of Engineers in charge of the clean up. The Bush EPA was a toothless tiger, and the Corps of Engineers, the other key player in the initiative, is worse. Not surprisingly, Baykeeper, Green Faith, and the Natural Resource Defense Council (NRDC) were forced, nearly four years ago, to bring legal action against the Corps; a case we won.

Only public outrage and local advocacy against Occidental's egregious dioxin pollution has so far resulted in decisive action. Not until Baykeeper, Hackensack Riverkeeper, and NRDC gave notice to Occidental of our intent to sue for "imminent endangerment" of human health and the environment did the EPA finally compel Occidental to pay for and expand the Superfund study area to include Newark Bay. We proved decisively in that moment that local muscle does work.

It became apparent to us early on that we would have more credibility as advocates if we didn't just battle the bad guys, but also were pro-active problem solvers. That's where our land conservation, and oyster restoration programs come into play. It was through a series of law suits—against operators of out of compliance combined sewers; against land owners preventing public access to our region's beaches and shorelines; against owners of contaminated land polluting our local waterways—that set the stage for our most important policy initiative. We gave people tools to understand their ownership of natural resources through our resurgent use of the ancient but still viable, Public Trust Doctrine. By changing public policy in both states through our *Brownfields to Greenfields* initiative, and most recently our policy initiative, has provided decision makers the tools to deal with stormwater and combined sewer overflow pollution through our work on Low Impact Development, a lower cost, low tech, green solution,

Baykeeper is a force to be reckoned with in urban land preservation. Today, as a result of our work, Baykeeper is a true partner with New Jersey's Green Acres program, the Port Authority, local communities, and urban open space advocates in finding the funds, and facilitating the transfer of important urban habitats from private to public management.

Ten years ago, I looked at a chart of the Navesink River, and saw that we were off Oyster Point in Red Bank. I came back to the office and said, "Let's get oysters back at Oyster Point." I was not only taken seriously, but the program started then is now 400-volunteer oyster gardeners strong—a bi-state program with oyster reefs restored, and a large scale benthic habitat restoration project on the way.

Another accomplishment I am most proud of is that Baykeeper is a founding member of the international Waterkeeper Alliance. Keepers are stubborn and audacious. These are good traits in a fight with polluters, but sometimes hard on the digestive system. When in 1994 seven of us tried to figure out how to form a national alliance of River, Sound and Baykeepers, sometimes we drank more Maalox than beer. But John Cronin, Terry Backer, Cynthia Poten, Mike Herz, Kenny Moser, Joe Payne, and I continued to come together in sometimes raucous, always exhausting meetings and had the impudence, the audacity, to start a national organization.

That dream, midwifed by John Cronin and Bobby Kennedy, and formalized in 1999, has since become the Waterkeeper Alliance, a worldwide movement of more than 180 Waterkeepers and growing. We started with a simple idea that continues to be our rallying cry today:

- Our rivers, bays, and sounds are the largest thing we will ever own.
- Water belongs to all of us and it is our right and responsibility to care for it.
- Everyone has a right to use our commonly owned natural resources, but no one has the right to use them to the detriment of anyone else.

The odds Waterkeepers face—small groups against huge polluters and reluctant, sometimes maleficent governments—are daunting. But our unique unifying strength as a movement arises from the very fact that we love such David and Goliath challenges. It's what gets us up in the morning, into the meeting rooms, and out on the water. It's also what makes a Waterkeeper in California, China, Columbia, Canada, or India able to stand up and say "I am the Waterkeeper," and make people listen, and makes things change.

HE IS NOT ALONE

George Ancona

John Cronin

I've had the good fortune to meet some wonderful people, who, like John, are dedicated to the preservation of the creatures with whom we share the Earth. By photographing and writing about these people for children's books, I have become aware of the plight of life on this planet. Here are three modified excerpts from the books, *Turtle Watch* (1987), *Man and Mustang* (1992), and *The Golden Lion Tamarin Comes Home* (1994). Let me introduce some of the people I've met in my journeys to produce these books.

Female turtle laying eggs

After surviving seventy million years of environmental upheaval, sea turtles are on the verge of extinction. During the nesting season, females leave the protective oceans and return to lay their eggs on the very same beaches where they were born. There she digs a hole and lays her eggs. After she covers the nest with sand, she lumbers back to the protective waves. The eggs are vulnerable to animal and human predators. Fishermen who live nearby can kill the helpless mother for meat and dig up the eggs. Both can be sold at the market.

TAMAR Group

On a remote beach on the northeast coast of Brazil there is a group of scientists who are working to save the sea turtles. The project is called TAMAR, which comes from the Portuguese name for the turtle, *Tartaruga marinha*. They are educating the fishermen about how the turtle's existence affects their livelihood.

Digging for eggs

Eggs in hat

When Rosa and Flavio, two children from the village, were poking about the beach they would look for the track of a mother Purtle returning to the ocean. They would then follow the track to the higher beach and begin to dig into the sand. There eggs are found and Rosa fills Flavio's straw hat with them.

Neca with Rosa and Flavio

Rosa with hatchling in hand

Hatching crawling on sand

The children take the eggs to Neca, one of the scientists with TAMAR. After Neca buries the eggs in a protected area, the children take her to where they found the eggs. There, Neca plants a pole with a number on it. Once the eggs are hatched they will take the hatchlings to the pole and release them from there.

Helicopter roundup of mustangs

Since the time of the Spanish *Conquistadores*, on the remote lands of our western states, herds of wild horses called mustangs roam. The mustangs are descendents of the Spanish horses, a breed created by the cross breeding of Arabian and Mongolian horses.

Erv Benally placing halter on mustang's head for the first time

Training wild mustang with rope and halter

Boy and father with adopted mustang

As the United States expanded, the horses were limited to areas that are now under the supervision of the Bureau of Land Management (BLM). These mustangs were originally killed or sold for dog food until the BLM established an Adopt-a-Horse program. Wild mustangs are now rounded up and taken to corrals adjacent to the New Mexico State penitentiary. There, prisoners volunteer to train the horses. Now, people who can demonstrate that they have a good place for a horse can adopt one.

Erv Benally is an experienced trainer. With patience and respect, he gentles[1] the mustang with strokes and talk until the horse accepts the halter. Day after day, Erv holds one end of the rope and patiently waits until the bucking and kicking is over. Eventually, the horse begins to trust the man and permits him to be led around. A family can buy a gentled mustang for $150.00. They will have to train the horse to the saddle, and after a while, a rider will be sitting tall in the saddle.

---

[1] "To gentle a horse" means to break it or tame it.

Golden Lion Tamarian

The Golden Lion Tamarin's habitat is the Mata Atlantica in Brazil. Deforestation has reduced the areas where tamarins live. The Golden Lion Tamarin Association (or the Associação Mico-Leão Dourado, AMLD) was formed in Brazil in November 1992 to administer and implement the Golden Lion Tamarin Conservation Program.[1] The friends I made in Brazil told me of the work being done to preserve the Golden Lion Tamarin. I thought it would be a great subject for another children's book. So off I went from Washington D.C to Rio de Janeiro and the Mata Atlantica.

The Golden Lion Tamarin Conservation Program strives to maximize the probability of survival of a naturally evolving population of GLTs; increase public awareness about GLTs; protect natural GLT habitat; and reintroduce captive-born tamarins back into their natural habitat in the Atlantic Coastal Rainforest of Southeastern Brazil[3].

[1] Previously administered by Dr. Benjamin Beck, of the Smithsonian's National Zoo, the Conservation Program was shifted to Brazil to consolidate administrative duties nearer to the center of the conservation action.
[3] Smithsonian National Zoological Park, Golden Lion Tamarian Conservation Program, http://nationalzoo.si.edu/ConservationAndScience/EndangeredSpecies//GLTProgram/GLTP/Mission

Dr. Benjamin Beck

The Golden Lion Tamarin Conservation Program recruits young, healthy tamarins that were born in zoos around the world and receives them in the National Zoo in Washington, D.C. There Dr. Benjamin Beck and his staff help prepare the young captive-born tamarins for their return to the wild.

The tamarins are allowed to run free in the zoo to accustom them to living in the wild. Each tamarin wears a radio collar that allows Dr. Beck and his associates to keep track of them as they scurry along fences and leap from tree to tree.

Andreia Martins in truck

In Brazil, Andreia Martins works with the Golden Tamarin Conservation Program. She and her observation crew pick up the tamarins on their arrival in Rio de Janeiro and take them to the Mata Atlantica rainforest.

Observer with antenna

Golden Lion Tamarian with collar

After a period of accilmating the tamarians to the new environment, researchers place radio collars on the tamarians and they are released in the wild.

Andreia with children

Today, they are flourishing and the farmers that used to cut down the rainforest now refer to them as my *micos*. [4] The program also talks to the townspeople and school children about preserving their trees and the *micos*.

---

[4] *Mico* is a small South American monkey (Mico melanurus), allied to the marmoset. The name was originally applied to an albino variety. Definition from Dictionary.com, http://dictionary.reference.com/browse/mico (accessed May 28, 2009).

A Meeting With A Remarkable Friend

The Rev. Canon Jeff Golliher

To honor my friend and colleague in this way is a privilege for which I am truly grateful. Several weeks ago, when I first sat down to write, I thought this would be the easiest thing in the world. I was wrong. The more I thought about what I might say, the more I realized the peculiar, but not totally unexpected dilemma that I faced. While it mainly brought a smile, it is a dilemma nonetheless. On the one hand, John Cronin's work to protect and care for the Hudson River and the body of life that it supports is legendary. In his case, we really are talking about a "living legend," and I am absolutely certain that he would not want me to say that. In fact, John would not want me to say very much about him at all. I can imagine him speaking these very words: "The work is not about personalities, so let's stay focused on the issues." He would be absolutely right. On the other hand, the exceptional nature of his character and passionate love for his work always draw out a personal response, as they should. The personal is part of his "gift" in the true vocational and spiritual sense of the word, and it would be a major mistake to overlook or ignore it here.

Having said that, let me qualify his imagined words by saying yes to "persons," and no to making this an issue of "personalities," "stars," and so on. As an anthropologist and priest in the Episcopal Church, I know as well as anyone that the personal dimension of existence is just as important as what we consider the "objective" to be. I say that very carefully. Many wise people have persuasively argued that the contentious, often confusing, and sometimes confused split between the two—subjectivity and objectivity, the personal and the impersonal—underlies much of the environmental crisis and the broader spiritual malaise that it represents. Speaking for myself, years of advanced training in the philosophy of science nurtured a genuine passion for "the facts" within me—which is precisely my point. Life is personal; the truths about life must be taken personally, if they have any lived meaning whatsoever; and the environmental crisis, which concerns everyone reading this volume, is exceedingly personal. Unless this crisis becomes personal for a great many more people very soon, Mother Earth will have no place for us, or no use for us. John knows this as well as anyone, probably better. My first conversation with him, years ago, which touched upon these very issues and forms the point of departure for this entire essay, illustrates just how personal the nature of the work we are honoring actually is. So, having explained myself and the reasoning behind what I have to say, I will do my best to respect the wishes of my friend. Beyond that, I trust that he will be forgiving.

I can't recall exactly when I first met John, perhaps it was a decade ago or more, but I remember the place. It was a small, conveniently located, outdoor cafe near Grand Central Station. More important than that, however, was my first impression of John, which I remember quite vividly. I realize that first impressions can be misleading. To know people, you have to spend time with them; even better, you have to walk in their shoes for a long distance. This was one of those exceptions that proves the rule: the more that I got to know John that day and thereafter, the more I realized just how true my first impression actually was.

The first thing I noticed was his utter sincerity, spiritual depth, and an exceptionally good sense of humor, which he readily applied to himself with grace and ease. Yet, these qualities, great as they are, are not what caught my attention the most. Rather, I was struck by how they seemed to weave together so seamlessly when he talked. The significance of this crystallized in my mind near the end of our lengthy conversation. The life of every person revolves around a love of some kind. We may hide it from others. We may hide it even from ourselves. What I realized was that John's love—for his vocation, his family, and life itself—which is hidden from no one, is somehow older than his bodily years can account for. I wouldn't call this an aspect of "personality" as psychologists might explain it. His love is expressed as a subtle, but perceptible presence that enters into John's whole being. Once you realize this, you can better appreciate how such a young man could have accomplished so much in the last thirty-five years. Then—and this is the best part—you wonder whether he's just beginning. I have no doubt that the answer is yes.

At the time, I had been "The Green Priest" at the Cathedral of St. John the Divine in Manhattan for nearly a decade; and John, as everyone knows, had been "The Riverkeeper" for much longer. Of course, given John's nature, he was not only "keeping" the Hudson, but also teaching people throughout the country how to get organized and care for their rivers. Although I suppose those respective roles were the more or less official reason for our meeting, the conversation that actually happened took a very different turn. John wanted to talk with someone in the church who saw the world from an ecological point of view. I wanted to talk with someone who had an ecological vocation that I thought would be a good model for the church. In effect, we wanted to look into each other's mirror, and we needed to understand what the other was seeing. It took only a matter of minutes to begin our inner, reflective "work" that day; and because of it, we became instant friends.

It was clear that both of us had been busy, probably too busy, for many years—but this wasn't the issue. We were trying to sort out the meaning of our lives and work during a turbulent time, and I'm not talking only about John and me as individuals. In the 80's and 90's, the country as a whole was turning in a decidedly conservative direction, politically, economically, and religiously—although the words "conservative" and "liberal" don't encompass enough meaning to account for the changes we were seeing. Some of the most significant, but subtle boundaries that give our culture its moral integrity were being crossed on a large scale. Aspects of the personal were becoming far too political; and aspects of the political, far too personal. In many churches, it was becoming more and more difficult to discern the difference between a political constituency and a gathering of the faithful. Adding insult to injury, a predictable, but disturbing "corporatizing" trend was moving through all parts of society, including large segments of the church. This was matched by a waning interest in grass-roots organizing and community development. Our society was choosing "top down," rather than "bottom up" solutions to any number of social, economic, and environmental ills, which we regarded as the same imposed, colonial mentality that had created those problems in the first place. In effect, real estate was taking priority over community— over the "human community and the earth community," as Thomas Berry would put it. The media was filled with propaganda rationalizing all this in the name of "free markets" as the paradigm of "freedom," while the prevailing ethos lurking just below the surface was greed—in effect, "take as much as you can, as quickly as you can, before the bottom falls out." It was one self-serving contradiction laid on top of another. Of course, that dreadful ethos spilled out across the whole planet; the bottom did fall out; and we've only begun to perceive the damage done to communities anywhere and everywhere. It may take a long time to dig ourselves out from under the mire.

It seems fitting and right to remember that conversation now. As a people, individually and together, we must learn to find that place within where we can gain even a glimpse of life's meaning and discover, or rediscover, what we need to be doing— that is, our spiritual vocations. Everyone has a vocation to heal our broken relation with the Earth, whether or not we're fortunate enough to live it as our "job." What matters the most is that we take the time to look for it, and then pursue it in whatever way that works. The answers we're looking for may not be revealed all at once. More likely, we'll meet up with unsettling, but terribly important questions—soul questions: What are we really trying to accomplish in life? What are the obstacles that we face? Are we creating them ourselves? What are our sorrows? And our joys? Those are the questions we were grappling with near Grand Central Station. It was an honest, realistic, and deeply spiritual conversation. We both understood that building an ecologically-rooted sense of community was at the heart of our vocation; yet, "the world" seemed to be moving in the opposite direction. The difference between the two and the struggle we had with it—and probably still have—was the reason for our meeting.

As it often happens in situations like this, our conversation delved into the past. We talked about our life histories in the context of the ecological worldview that emerged in the 1960s and 70s. Our thoughts turned to some of the debates that raged in those days. Notable among them was Lynn White's famous article in *Science* called "The Spiritual Roots of the Ecological Crisis."[1] White placed a large part of the blame for the crisis on Western religion, specifically the church, arguing that the basic values of stewardship and responsibility for "this world" had been forsaken by otherworldly concerns. His widely-read article was followed by a book, *A God Within*,[2] authored by Rene Dubos, the eminent microbiologist from Rockefeller University. Dubos countered White by reminding his readers of the ecological worldview on which the Franciscan and Benedictine movements had been founded. Although both scientists offered different points of view, they both argued persuasively that spiritual values were found at the heart of the environmental crisis, both in its causes and its solutions.

The irony in this debate was that, at about the same time, the World Council of Churches (WCC) strongly criticized—and justifiably so—the environmental movement as being disconnected from the spiritual roots of the crisis that it wanted to solve. Representatives of the WCC from the developing and least-developed nations, said that "environmentalism," as it was understood in the West, overlooked the deeper patterns of economic exploitation and injustice that had impoverished people and the planet for centuries; and about this, most churches had spoken clearly and often, as they still do. In effect, the WCC was saying that the crisis we face is not "environmental," not if by that we mean "our surroundings." The laws of nature have not changed. Ecological systems, which we are part of, still work according to the same principles. The crisis we face is thoroughly

[1] Lynn Townsend White, Jr, "The Historical Roots of Our Ecologic Crisis," *Science*, 155 (March 10, 1967): 1203–1207.
[2] Rene Dubos, *A God Within* (New York: Scribner Book Company, 1973).

human. They were thinking of some ancient vices, like greed and pride, "legalized" theft (the taking of land and resources that are not ours to take), and the delusional self-righteousness that rationalizes it, often in the name of "the good." My guess is that nearly fifty years later, we still have trouble understanding that "the environment" is not entirely separate from us, and that the ultimate causes of "the crisis" will not be found "out there," but within ourselves. From time to time, we all need to look into that inner, self-reflective mirror where we find our vocations and true selves. Now, at this critical turning point in history, is definitely the time to begin or to begin again.

We talked well into the afternoon mainly about what was eventually called "sustainable communities." Looking back, I would say we were exploring the principle of "ecological embodiment" that characterizes the spiritual meaning of "sustainability." Rather than moving in the direction of increasingly disembodied virtual worlds, we must learn to live in the here and now again, *and want to live there*, if there is any hope of adopting an ecologically sustainable way of life. We were reflecting on our bodies and whole selves as part of families, households, communities, and bioregions—all these individual and collective bodies interwoven in the one great body of life. We may try to live in "other worlds"—for example, in a world where environmental exploitation is believed to have no consequence or cost—but it is in our flesh and blood, our ecological existence that we find our primary spiritual reality. It is there, that is to say, "here," where we find life's meaning. Not only that, ecological embodiment applies to institutions just as much as it does to individuals and communities. Human institutions like the church, the university, brokerage houses, and corporations must be re-created as extensions of the web of life, rather than the interlocking but collectively disembodied webs of political and economic relationships that currently define their primary purpose. In the end, as in the beginning, it all becomes very personal—the struggle for meaning, the need for community, a feel for the sacred, and the instinct for survival wrap around each other within the soul of every person.

It was at this point in the conversation that we shared some bits and pieces of our lives in the form of stories. For me, this involved the sometimes circuitous route that my life had taken in terms of geography and vocation: from the Blue Ridge Mountains in North Carolina to Manhattan (and now the Catskills) via Central America and Europe, and from academics and extensive fieldwork as a cultural anthropologist to the priesthood and the church. John and I both knew how important it is to remember our lives: where we're from, what we've actually done, and what we're meant to be doing. The telling of personal stories can be a significant step toward healing the split between nature and culture within the soul of the individual and the collective soul of families and communities—even nations. This split is deeply rooted in our selves, and in our whole culture, which are the selves and the culture that we must transform. By sharing a story of this kind with you here—a story about my great-grandfather, water, and me—I believe I've found a way to honor John's wishes: I can reveal something about the personal nature of this work, without focusing too much on him or making the desire to honor him an issue of personalities—especially his.

Anyone who has ever visited the mountains just west of the Hudson—the Catskills and the Shawangunks—knows how fortunate I am to live there. My wife, Asha, and I left Manhattan nearly five years ago. After fifteen years of city life, you would have thought that a lengthy period of adjustment would have been necessary. It wasn't—maybe twenty-four hours was all I needed. Probably less. Having been raised in a relatively poor, way off the beaten path, small town in the Blue Ridge, moving to the Catskills was like going back home. I love the mountains and the water, especially the rapids of small streams flowing into deep pools; and I love fly fishing. Flowing water and a fly rod do something to still my busy mind and make my soul rest easy, which means that standing in a stream is a spiritual experience. Of course I would say that, being a priest and all. I suppose it justifies (some would say "rationalizes") my love for fly fishing. But I would argue that standing in a mountain stream—feeling the breeze against my face and the cool water curling around my legs—is one form that holy communion can take. No, it's not that I "would," argue that. I actually do, routinely and often.

Apparently, my affinity for water was passed down to me from my great-grandfather, Joel. He was a simple *and* a complex man. He had the brightest, kindest light in his eyes that you would ever see in a human face; yet his well-known stubborn disposition confirmed the unfortunate stereotype of Appalachian folk as difficult people. As contradictory as this sounds, both qualities were profoundly embodied in him. He was a real character, and I loved him. Everyone did. He was a man of few words. In his younger days, he lived in a log cabin and pursued his livelihood as a small farmer. The only time I ever saw him wear anything other than bib-overalls and a white shirt was at funerals. I'm inclined to say that he wore his brown suit to church too, but I won't—I don't believe he ever went to church except at funerals.

My great-grandfather didn't fish, but he was a dowser. I don't really know how people feel about things like dowsing these days, or whether they even know what it is. Speaking for myself, I don't have a strong opinion, one way or another, about its scientific validity. Yet I think we all understand that traditional folk have great wisdom about the land, livelihood, and the greater meaning of life that we, apparently, still struggle with. Because this wisdom has been tragically denied in the past, I want to make a quick detour in my story. The detour begins with religion and the soul; it ends with knowledge and the Earth.

Most everyone knows that as late as the 19th and 20th centuries, Europeans and Americans commonly believed that the sacred teachings of so-called "primitive people" do not constitute "true" religion. Not being Christian, I suppose, made them seem superstitious, childish, and unequipped intellectually to take care of their own souls. I would like to think that we, as a people, have forever outgrown such terrible prejudice, but I know we haven't, not completely. The rise of religious fundamentalism everywhere testifies to how much growing we still have to do. Sometimes I wonder whether the same can be said for beliefs about environmental stewardship. In recent years, even some anthropologists have fought over this very question: Do indigenous peoples have "true" ecological knowledge? This is an unusually complex and controversial question. I try to look at it from the standpoint of indigenous peoples themselves, who can be very practical, just as my great-grandfather was a practical man. Think of it this way. If our answer is anything close to resembling "no"—meaning that our knowledge is better than theirs—then one possible and perhaps likely consequence will be this: We will tell ourselves that because the environmental crisis is really bad (which is true), it would be best for us, the possessors of "true" ecological knowledge, to take care of their land for them—for the sake of everyone. In response, the First Peoples say: And then, at the end of this age, when the dust finally settles, who will "own" the land? Who actually will take care of it? Who will have a decent livelihood and a sustainable way of life? Even more, who will be alive and who will be dead? Setting aside significant methodological and other differences between "modern science" and "folk science," you have to ask yourself whether we're still living in colonial times called by another name, our penchant for colonizing being employed in contemporary ways. Two hundred years ago, the issue was the care of the soul; today, it's the care of the Earth. Our scientific knowledge is more sophisticated and refined than it was in the past, our spiritual vision considerably enlarged, and our good intentions just as well-intended, but the underlying political and economic interests—and the *hubris*—that undergird them still loom very large, with the potential for the same treacherous impact.

So with that in mind, let's return to my great-grandfather, the dowser. When a furniture factory was being built in our small town, the engineers could not find water anywhere on the grounds, despite the fact that the factory was located on the edge of a large riverbed. The river itself was probably less than a quarter mile away. Reluctantly, they called Joel. He cut a forked stick, and soon thereafter, told them where to drill, which they did. They found plenty of water—more than enough. Years later, I spent a lot time by the small company reservoir that was his legacy. I held a fishing pole there for the first time and began to understand who my great-grandfather was—and who I was.

That gives you an impression of what he was like and my love for him, but it was the look in his eyes I really want to tell you about. Actually, I have in mind one particular look that I saw on one particular day. I'll never forget it. It was a Sunday afternoon. Our whole family—four generations of us—ate lunch together on Sundays. Every Sunday. I'm not kidding or exaggerating. We had fried chicken, the best homemade biscuits you've ever eaten, greens cooked with bacon, mashed potatoes, and iced tea every Sunday afternoon; and throughout each and every meal, my great-grandfather sat at the head of the table and rarely said a word. He smiled a lot though. Mainly, he spoke through his eyes.

About the time I was old enough to walk through the furniture factory with my grandfather (who was the plant supervisor), I developed the habit of asking probing questions at the dinner table. On that one particular Sunday, I was wondering about the varnishing and staining materials that the factory used. I knew they smelled bad. I had seen the fans and the workmen wearing protective masks. Both my grandfather and father carefully instructed me to stay away from the fumes, because they were poisonous. I did as they said. What I wanted to know, and asked at the dinner table, was this: Where were those materials disposed? Where did they go? I can't recall exactly why I raised the question, not at that moment, but I do remember thinking of the river in the distance, the fields of corn on the flood plain, and the farms. I was an inquisitive child, and my question was perfectly innocent. I just wanted to know.

A silent, void-like emptiness filled the room, which startled me at first. It was obvious that no one knew the answer. I assumed, rightly I believe, that no one had thought about it very much. This was long before Congress had written the bulk of our environmental laws and regulations, and before courses in ecology or environmental science were taught in public schools. As usual, my great-grandfather said nothing. It wasn't necessary. His eyes said it all. The twinkle we all adored shifted to a different wavelength—more focused and powerful, to say the very least. You would have thought that the presence of God had descended into the center of our dinner table, and the message that I heard was loud and clear: *What did you say? Has someone poisoned the well? Have we forgotten that water is sacred? Do you realize that poisoning the well is an act of war?* He wasn't "talking" only about "his well," the one he discovered years before with a forked stick and uncanny intuition, after the engineers had failed. His eyes were telling me about the meaning of any well, any source or body of water, anywhere. From his point of view, the fact that none of us knew the answer to my question was already sufficient evidence that a serious moral line had been crossed. Around our dinner table on one ordinary Sunday afternoon, the spiritual foundation of the cosmos that I knew was shaking quite a lot. I learned how powerful questions can be, and I witnessed how forcefully the universe can answer through the actions of just one person.

It would be wrong for me to imply that people in our small town were negligent or reckless in these matters. They cared a lot about the well-being of the land and of their families, friends, and neighbors. The factory was family-owned, deeply rooted in the community, and the people who made a living within its walls were highly skilled—many were true artists who could make a chair from scratch. My point: they knew a great deal about "sustainable communities," years before those words were ever spoken or debated. As in all small towns, people in ours had their own way of going about things. Usually, they listened and responded without saying much or creating a fuss. What I always remember is that a couple of years after that fateful Sunday, when I was learning the ropes on my first summer job in the factory, a lot of people working there had become quite knowledgeable about issues of human health and environmental protection—and they made it clear to me that they knew what they were talking about. They were proud people, who took great pride in their work. I can't say, nor would I want to say, that my innocent question or my great-grandfather's wisdom were behind all this. Nevertheless, what I heard and saw that summer was impressive, even for a child.

It should go without saying that this story has great meaning for me, simple as it is. Yet, few things are simple these days, and what appears to be simple often turns out to be simple-minded or self-serving. We live in an age of innuendo, spin, gossip that passes for news, and deception that passes for truth. Seemingly simple solutions to serious problems usually amount to calculated avoidance or denial, which not only steers public policy in the wrong direction, but also conceals the hard truths we need to know. For those reasons among many others, I would be among the first to cast my vote for diversity and complexity. And for the same reasons, I can imagine that some readers might ask whether it's possible for a simple look to express so much, so plainly. I'll tell you straight out that it certainly is possible. At the risk of appearing naïve, I think my great-grandfather was expressing the kind of tacit, traditional knowledge that ordinary people, the vast majority of humankind, have always known and valued, unless they're brainwashed into believing something else. They have known this—*Do not poison the well!*—because survival depends on it. Sacred knowledge of this kind is, above all, practical. It brings together our primeval instinct for survival with a higher awareness of the sacred in the most intricate and intimate way. This should go without saying too—poisoning the well cannot possibly, under any circumstances, be regarded as an acceptable way of doing business, or living a life. To make it seem acceptable is to rationalize the consequences that must inevitably follow: destruction, illness, even death. An equivalent kind of traditional knowledge might be something like, *don't put your hand in a rattlesnake den!* Or, *don't put someone else's hand in a rattlesnake den!* Who in their right mind could ever believe this wasn't true? Or act as if it wasn't true? I suppose my great-grandfather must have wondered if the next generation— meaning "our generation"—might be losing its mind and its soul; and in his own irrepressible way, he let us know exactly what he thought.

It was many years later that John and I spoke of the environmental and spiritual necessity of creating sustainable communities, which will require a tremendous transformation in our way of life. The task is daunting. The transformation we need goes deep and it is urgent; but ultimately, its success depends on the gradual accumulation of small changes—one person, one family, one community, one nation at a time—until a crucial threshold is finally reached. What I know, first-hand, is that something as small as a simple look in a person's eyes can be enough to take someone else across that threshold. For a few precious moments, that simple and complex man, a poor dirt farmer with no formal education, raised the consciousness of four generations eating fried chicken around the dinner table on a Sunday afternoon. In ways that were too subtle to be fully perceived or easily explained, he enlarged our understanding, changed our behavior, and planted a seed in my soul that shaped the course that my life would eventually take. All this he did in the twinkle of an eye.

When I think of him today, I don't see him as a figure from the past—an icon of bygone days, forever lost. Rather, I wonder what he would say if he were with us now. First, I believe he would tell us to strengthen our environmental laws even more and enforce them more carefully, so we might better remember what was once written in our hearts—and why it was written there. This is a moral and public responsibility on the highest order of human existence. Second, he would say that we also have a deeper calling, which is to write in our hearts, clearly and plainly, what we have had no choice but to write into our laws. This is our spiritual responsibility and our birthright as persons made in God's image. Our vocation is not one or the other, but both; and both are exceedingly personal.

We have come a long way. I know that my great-grandfather wasn't speaking for science, or the law, or religion that Sunday afternoon. He knew very little about those things; and back then, the churches in his part of the world were on the sidelines of any serious discussion of the environment. Today, I'm glad to say that this has changed, and that the laws have changed, and that "ecology" has become a household word. When I think of him now, I'm not remembering the past as much as renewing my hope for the future. In his eyes, I see the brightness of the next generation and the next. I want them to be here, alive and well on God's green Earth, for their sake and ours; I want them to learn from our mistakes and from our successes; and I want them to look upon us favorably.

That's why I'm always searching for that same bright and sometimes fiery look in the eyes of people I meet. It's a sign of all kinds of good things: inspiration and hope, faith and courage, and enough never-give-up determination to carry us through these difficult times. One day, not very long ago, I saw it in someone, a friend that I had only just met. We were sitting in a place that's about as far from southern Appalachia as you can imagine. Like I said, we were in a cafe near Grand Central Station. I love both places, and I loved that look in his eyes. It seems like such a small thing, but I know it's not. It can change the world.

Fighting Fatalism About War

John Horgan

Every Halloween, John Cronin and his wife, Connie Hough throw a party for parents of kids trick-or-treating in Cold Spring. John and I often get into inappropriately earnest arguments at these affairs. Last Halloween the topic was my belief that humanity will soon stop fighting wars. John, as I recall—and I wasn't drinking that night, so I'm pretty confident in my recollection—reacted skeptically to my optimistic vision. I would thus like to lay out my case with more care in this essay. Although I probably won't change John's mind—he's impossibly stubborn, a quality that has served him well as an environmental activist—I might get through to others reading these essays.

I've been doing research on and writing about war—from raids of hunter-gatherers to global nuclear war—throughout my career as a science journalist. My interest mutated into an obsession in the aftermath of 9/11, when I gradually noticed that most people are extremely fatalistic about war. A dinner discussion with five fellow science journalists just after the U.S. invasion of Iraq was typical. When I revealed my hopes for a warless and largely demilitarized world, my colleagues smiled and shook their heads, as if I had professed belief in angels or astrology. Every one felt that war between nations is inevitable. Since then I've taken every opportunity—on the Internet, during lectures, at conferences and parties, in restaurants and taxis—to ask people of all ages and backgrounds whether they think war will ever be abolished. More than nine people in ten give me the same answer: war will never end.

In 2006 I began teaching a class called "War and Human Nature" at Stevens Institute of Technology, an engineering school in New Jersey. On the first day of class, I asked the sixteen students whether they thought war will ever end. Eleven said no, five yes. Some of those who answered yes, I realized later, were just telling the professor what they thought he wanted to hear; only two students turned out to be genuine optimists.

As an assignment, I had my students ask classmates: "Will humans ever stop fighting wars, once and for all? Why or why not?" Of the 205 respondents, 185, over 90%, replied "No." The justifications were diverse: "We're naturally evil people." "People are always going to hate and try to destroy 'inferiors.'" "Monkeys fight with each other and because humans are animals too we follow that pattern." "Men are power crazy and women are not in power." "People would just get bored with no war."

Young people have less faith now than they did decades ago, if previous surveys are any guide. In 1987, the psychologist David Adams of Wesleyan University polled 126 students on whether "wars are inevitable because human beings are naturally aggressive." Only 33% of the students agreed with this statement, and only 40% believed that "war is intrinsic to human nature." These results resemble those obtained in similar surveys of 327 students in Finland in 1984 and of 5,000 students in 18 nations in 1969.[1]

The current wave of pessimism is all too understandable, given 9/11 and all its bloody sequelae, not to mention conflicts roiling the Middle East, Central Africa and other troubled regions. Moreover, recent research into the roots of human conflict seems, at first glance, to support the notion that war is "in our genes," as my students put it. As far back as scientists have looked into human pre-history, they have found evidence of lethal group fighting. The anthropologist Lawrence Keeley of the University of Illinois estimates that more than ninety percent of pre-state, tribal societies engaged in at least occasional warfare, and many fought constantly. Tribal combat usually involved skirmishes and ambushes rather than pitched battles, but over time the fighting could produce mortality rates as high as 50 %.[2]

[1] All statements from 1987 paper by Adams and Bosch; available by author on request.
[2] Lawrence H. Keeley, *War Before Civilization* (New York: Oxford University Press, 1996).

These findings, the Harvard archaeologist Steven LeBlanc contends, demolish the claim of the 18th-century French philosopher Jean-Jacques Rousseau, that prior to civilization humans were naturally compassionate and lived in harmony with each other and with nature. Primeval warfare, LeBlanc asserts, stemmed from a fierce, Malthusian struggle for food and other resources. "Since the beginning of time," he explains, "humans have been unable to live in ecological balance. No matter where we happen to live on Earth, we eventually outstrip the environment. This has always led to competition as a means of survival, and warfare has been the inevitable consequence of our ecological-demographic propensities."[3]

Some scientists now trace warfare all the way back to the common ancestor we shared with chimpanzees, our closest genetic relatives. Beginning in the mid-1970s, researchers in Tanzania and elsewhere have observed male chimpanzees from the same troop banding together to patrol their territory; if they encounter a chimp from a different troop, the raiders beat him, often to death. Mortality rates from intergroup violence among chimpanzees, the Harvard anthropologist Richard Wrangham reports, are roughly comparable to rates observed among human hunter-gatherers.

"Chimpanzee-like violence preceded and paved the way for human war," Wrangham asserts, "making modern humans the dazed survivors of a continuous, five-million-year habit of lethal aggression." Wrangham contends that male primates "evolved to possess strong appetites for power, because with extraordinary power comes extraordinary reproductive success." As evidence, he points to warrior leaders like Genghis Khan, who sired thousands of offspring.[4]

In spite of all these grim findings, most authorities on the origins of warfare reject the fatalistic notion that war is

---

[3] Steven A. LeBlanc, *Constant Battles: The Myth of Peaceful, Noble Savage* (New York: St. Martin's Press 2003), p. XIV.

[4] Richard Wrangham and Dale Peterson, *Demonic Males* (London: Bloombury-Publishing, 1997), 63, 233.

an inevitable consequence of our biology. The anthropologist Jonathan Haas of the University of Chicago points out that rates of warfare have always fluctuated both between and within societies, contradicting the "preposterous" notion that warfare is so innate that it is inevitable. "If war is deeply rooted in our biology, then it's going to be there all the time," Haas argues. "And it's just not." War, Haas adds, is certainly not innate in the same sense as language, which has been exhibited by all known human societies at all times.[5]

The anthropologists Carolyn and Melvin Ember agree that biological theories cannot explain patterns of warfare among either pre-state or state societies. The Embers oversee Yale University's Human Relations Area Files, a database of information on some 360 cultures past and present. More than ninety percent of these societies have engaged in warfare, but some societies fight constantly and others rarely, while a few have never been observed fighting. The Embers have found correlations between rates of warfare and environmental factors, notably droughts, floods and other natural disasters that provoke fears of famine.[6]

Even scientists whose work seems to support fatalism toward war dismiss that attitude themselves. One is the anthropologist Napoleon Chagnon of the University of California at Santa Barbara, who is renowned for finding a link between male violence and reproductive success among the Yanomamo, a warlike tribal Amazonian society he has studied since the 1960s. According to Chagnon, Yanomamo killers have, on average, twice as many wives and three times as many children as non-killers. But Chagnon has always denied that Yanomamo males fight because of a "war gene" or instinct. Truly compulsive, out-of-control killers, Chagnon notes, are quickly killed themselves. Successful warriors are usually quite calculating, he says; they fight because that is how a male advances in their society. Moreover, many Yanomamo men have confessed to Chagnon that they loathe war and wish it could be abolished from their culture—and, in fact, rates of violence have recently dropped

[5] Personal Communication
[6] Personal Communication

dramatically, as Yanomamo villages have accepted the laws and mores of the outside world[7]

History offers many other examples of warlike societies that rapidly became peaceful. Vikings were the scourge of Europe during the Middle Ages, but their Scandinavian descendants are among the most peaceful people on Earth. Similarly, Germany and Japan, which just seventy years ago were the world's most militaristic, aggressive nations, have embraced pacifism, albeit after catastrophic defeats.

In fact, contrary to the impression created by newspaper headlines, humanity as a whole is much less warlike than it used to be. In other words: Things are getting better! World Wars I and II and all the other horrific conflicts of the 20th century resulted in the deaths of fewer than three percent of the global population. That is an order of magnitude less than the rate of violent death for males in the average primitive society, whose weapons consisted only of clubs and spears rather than machine guns and bombs.[8]

Conventional wars between the armies of two or more nations have decreased sharply over the past half century, and major civil wars have declined since peaking in the early 1990s. Most conflicts now consist of guerilla wars, insurgencies and terrorism—or what the political scientist John Mueller of Ohio State University calls the "remnants of war." Mueller rejects biological explanations for the trend, since "testosterone levels seem to be as high as ever." Noting that democracies rarely if ever wage war against each other, Mueller attributes the decline of warfare over the past fifty years at least in part to a surge in the number of democracies around the world—from twenty to almost one-hundred.[9]

The Harvard psychologist Steven Pinker identifies several other possible reasons for the recent decline of warfare and other forms of violence: First, the creation of stable states with effective

---

[7] Personal Communication

[8] Keeley, *War Before Civilization.*

[9] John Mueller, "The Demise of War and of Speculations About the Causes Thereof," National Convention of the International Studies Association Chicago, Illinois, February 26-March 4, 2007. Available from http://polisci.osu.edu/faculty/jmueller/ISA2007W.PDF (accessed June 24, 2009).

legal systems and police forces has eliminated the Hobbesian anarchy of all against all. Second, our increased life expectancies make us less willing to risk our lives by engaging in violence. Third, as a result of globalization and communications, we have become increasingly interdependent on—and empathetic toward—others outside of our immediate tribes.[10]

In short, many lines of research contradict the myth that war is a constant of the human condition. These studies also suggest that—contrary to the myth of the peaceful, noble savage— civilization has not created the problem of warfare; it is helping us solve it. We need more civilization, not less, if we wish to eradicate war. Civilization has given us legal institutions that resolve disputes by establishing laws, negotiating agreements and enforcing them. These institutions, which range from local courts to the United Nations, have vastly reduced the risk of violence both within and between nations.

Obviously, our institutions are far from perfect. Nations around the world still maintain huge arsenals, including weapons of mass destruction, and armed conflicts still ravage many regions. So what should we do? The anthropologist Melvin Konner of Emory proposes female education as one key to reducing conflict. Many studies, he notes, have demonstrated that an increase in the education of females leads to a decrease in birth rates. The result is a stabilized population, which decreases demands on governmental and medical services and depletion of natural resources and hence the likelihood of social unrest. A lower birth rate also reduces what some demographers call "bare branches"—unmarried, unemployed young men, who are associated with higher rates of violent conflict both within and between nations. "Education of girls is by far the best investment you can make in a developing country," Konner says.[11]

In my "War and Human Nature" course at Stevens, we discuss other ways to promote peace, such as decreasing severe poverty and ensuring a more equitable distribution of food, water and other resources; developing cheap, clean, renewable sources

[10] Steven Pinker, "A History of Violence," *The New Republic Online* (March 20, 2007), http://pinker.wjh.harvard.edu/articles/media/2007_03_19/Newpercent20Republic.pdf (accessed June 24, 2009).
[11] Personal communication

of energy; and bolstering the power of the United Nations to anticipate and quell outbreaks of violence and keep the peace. No single solution will be sufficient in and of itself. War seems to be over-determined, springing from many different causes, not all of which are necessary for war to occur. Peace, if it is to last, must be over-determined too.

The Harvard biologist Edward O. Wilson, the great champion of biodiversity, is confident that we will find ways to cease making war on nature as well as on each other. "I'm optimistic about saving biodiversity," he told me recently.[12] "And I think that once we face the problems underlying the origins of tribalism and religious extremism—face them frankly and look for the roots—then we'll find a solution to those too in terms of an informed international negotiation system."

The causes of peace and conservation are mutually reinforcing. Remember the old Vietnam-era poster that said, "War is bad for children and other living things"? All living things will benefit once we humans stop diverting so much of our energy and resources into fighting and preparing for wars. And the first step toward ending war is to believe that we can end it.

[12] Personal communication

LIVING INTO A THEOLOGY OF CREATION

Jim Heron

*"Then God said, 'Let us make man in our image, after our
likeness; and let them have dominion over the fish of the sea,
and over the birds of the air, and over the cattle, and over all the
earth, and over every creeping thing that creeps upon the earth.'"*
Genesis 1:26 [NRSV]

"... and let them have dominion..." sounds as if God gave
humankind a great deal, doesn't it? However, my fascination
with this portion of Scripture, which is held sacred by
Christian, Jewish and Muslim peoples alike, is undergirded by
my understanding that to *have dominion* also means to have
responsibility for caring for the Earth, for contributing to its
health, and for being, in general, a good steward of Creation.
In over forty years of active ministry as an Episcopal priest, I
was given countless opportunities to teach good stewardship
of Creation and to appreciate the variety of ways parishioners
of all ages then chose to engage in living into their "dominion."
I remember young children in the Church School coming with
their parents to help at parish clean-up days especially when we
were given the gift of the gorgeous spring or fall weather typical
in the Hudson Valley and hunkering down over the entrance to
the burrow dug by one of God's creatures under the sidewalk
asking: Who lives here? Can we keep him safe even when people
need to walk by here all the time? What does it eat...we don't
want to clear its food away with the rakes and shovels, do we?
Old timers in the parish sincerely hoped that the skunk residing
in that hole would remain within while the children were
close by! Those parishioners past the initial stages of youthful

wonder in the gift of Creation puzzled over how to coexist with the multitude of mosquito-eating bats living in the church attic and depositing pounds of nutrient-rich guano that threatened the integrity of the ceiling even as they marveled at the bats swooping out from under the eaves at dusk after the evening services. At every turn, the needs of humankind and those of the many other parts of Creation must be held in a delicate and deliberately-considered balance. This is the wide-ranging understanding shared by many at Beacon Institute for Rivers and Estuaries (BIRE), including John Cronin. Observing that this understanding led to passionate action by both staff and management led me to search for ways to put my hands to work in support of the theology of Creation when I retired in 2003 from parish ministry. I have found new life volunteering alongside people whose passion for environmental concerns guides their very being; it has awakened dormant parts of my soul.

I met John Cronin on my very first visit to this center, when it was newly established in Beacon by Governor George Pataki. I had heard the Governor's State of the State Address in 2000 and was excited by the vision he proposed for a Rivers and Estuaries Center. I had followed with great interest the search for a proper site and was delighted when Beacon was chosen. When the news hit the local papers, I immediately felt a whole-hearted inside pull toward and into different and, as yet undefined, ways to contribute to the stewardship of Creation. As it turned out, my gifts as a storyteller, speaker, and teacher were about to be put to fresh use. At the time I knew nothing about John's work on the Hudson River, nor was I familiar with his leadership in measures to protect it. I didn't even know that there was such a thing as a "Riverkeeper." What did become immediately clear was that we were both working from only slight variations of the same script. We shared a sense of the sacredness of the environment and zeal both for immersing our own hands and for educating others so that they, too, would yearn to play a part.

It was not long after this first meeting that John asked if I would research and design a pamphlet on the history of Denning's Point, the site of BIRE. Such astounding events and stories of fantastically extraordinary people came to light in the process of my research that the whole BIRE staff (a mere four of us at the time) realized we were in the throes of giving birth to a book rather than a short pamphlet. It was John who first envisioned the Denning's Point historical project serving as a paradigm for almost any waterfront site on the Hudson. The lessons we learned from a close examination of the Point's specific history would open eyes to the various uses and abuses of Creation found up and down the Hudson River. John's vision excited me and served to sustain me as I began what quickly became a very personal journey into the history of Denning's Point. The search was intense. Hours spent tediously examining and painstakingly seeking were interspersed with moments of sheer ecstasy as yet another secret gave way to the exultation of an "ah ha" moment. As we pored over the historical evidence I uncovered, John and I realized we share the conviction that future possibility is illuminated and supported by knowledge of the past of Denning's Point.

As we grew into this conviction, the journey into the history of Denning's Point became much more than an educational exercise for my brain; it quickly became intensely personal and spiritual, engaging my entire physical being, heart and soul. My previous work within the environmental movement was focused on global concerns, but I had never immersed myself to the point of "getting down and dirty" with issues surrounding clean water, renewable energy, recycling, or any other noble cause in need of more champions. It was immediately different with my exploration of Denning's Point. When I was searching for historical tidbits in libraries and sifting through the dusty archives of the American Museum of Natural History and the New York State Museum, or kneeling on her earth carefully uncovering her prehistoric and historic treasures, or just standing on her outermost point with the waves lapping on her shore, Denning's Point was speaking to me, always inviting me to know her better. As I walked her bounds day after day, I found myself profoundly touched in ways I had never imagined. It was as if the Island had become a living, breathing entity that whispered her past to me and to anybody else who cared enough to listen.

It was when I became aware that prehistoric people had

settled on the Point that the whispering began. Those early inhabitants took care of the land that, in turn, sustained them; I reveled in this part of the island's history listening within myself to the life lessons offered to all of us in the present day. The prehistoric inhabitants and the subsequent Native Americans were good stewards of the environment taking only what they truly needed and leaving the land essentially as they had found it. As I rambled over, around, and through this sixty-four acre piece of Creation soaking in the implications of these revelations, I heard the whispers of the Point's past. "I could imagine the rustle of migrant hunters, the laughter of children around ancient campfires, the sound of a craftsman honing a point. They seemed so clean and simple, their lives not yet sullied by civilization."[1] You can imagine the reaction of BIRE staff when I first shared this startling revelation about "hearing voices." Only John understood exactly what I was speaking about and was willing to say so, standing alongside without fear of what others might think. His long love of the Hudson River, born of many hours spent on her waters, had made the river as alive to him as Denning's Point was becoming to me.

As the history of Denning's Point unfolded, John and I discovered many instances in which her history and that of the Hudson River were intertwined. One morning as I was voicing my deep indignation about the filth and abuse of the river that surrounded Denning's Point, John cross-referenced my indignation with his own study of the desecration as cited in one of his many writings. "As early as the 1870s, Harper's Weekly had featured a regular editorial commentary on the state of the river in the form of a white-bearded cartoon character called Father Hudson, who would complain about the filth plaguing the lower river."[2] John has always been as passionate when speaking about the river as he is when writing about the river; it is truly a passion we share for our respective "beloveds." John and I have found grounds for numerous similar discussions as the stories of Denning's Point and the tales of the Hudson

[1] Jim Heron, *Denning's Point, A Hudson River History* (Hensonville, NY: Black Dome Press, 2006), 25.

[2] John Cronin and Robert F. Kennedy, Jr., *The Riverkeepers* (New York, NY: Simon & Schuster, 1999), 55.

River crossed paths. As the history of Denning's Point revealed itself, John began incorporating it into his vast understanding of the Hudson and thereby became a steady source of support as I sought to unlock further historical mysteries of Denning's Point.

One of the more extraordinary revelations in the search to uncover the details of the history of Denning's Point was that Alexander Hamilton had lived on the Point and had written a number of significant historical documents while in residence. These documents were influential in the writing of both the Constitution of the United States of America and the framework of our national fiscal system. It was fascinating to read Hamilton's own words as he explicated his system for bolstering American credit, including the necessity of founding a national bank. From Denning's Point, Alexander Hamilton penned his famous line, "A national debt, if it is not excessive, will be to us a national blessing. It will be powerful cement of our Union."[3] As was so often the case in our work together, while I was joyfully focusing on the immediate and local historical implications of this important discovery, John took it to the next level noting its larger and more visionary importance. We were equally excited, but for markedly different reasons. John supported my discovery and made sure that it received the attention of Governor Pataki's office. He and I had the opportunity to share one of many grins as we both recognized the irony of a question posed to us by the governor's office before releasing news of the discovery to the press: Is the Hamilton story "bullet proof?" While the revelation regarding Alexander Hamilton's writings did prove to be bullet proof, Alexander himself was not; he had been killed in a pistol duel with Aaron Burr. Remembering this interchange still brings a smile to my face.

While John and I are very different people seeing with distinctly individualized eyes, our respective passion for Creation and our sense of duty to take care of it override the relatively small personal variations on the theme. When John is on a boat on his beloved river, or expanding upon his visionary hopes for

[3] Heron, *Denning's Point, A Hudson River History,* 55.

the future, or talking about the future of the Hudson River, he shines at his charismatic best. I know what that feels like, for I share that explosion of zeal when talking about or walking on Denning's point. I shall be always grateful to John Cronin for the chance to research the history and become the storyteller for Denning's Point. While learning about Denning's Point I fell in love and like all lovers will enthuse eagerly about any aspect pertaining to the object of my affection, but especially regarding environmental stewardship and its place in my ever-growing appreciation for and understanding of the theology of Creation.

ON <u>TRUST</u>[1]

Anthony DePalma

A big part of confronting the challenges of the environment—whether by doing something about it or by writing about those who are doing something about it—is knowing what to watch out for. Sounds simple, I know. But it is the most basic, and most pervasive, of all the guidelines you will ever run into. I can say this because both in my own personal life and in my professional career as a writer and reporter on the environment, I have been constantly reminded of how much I don't know.

Back when I was young and the first car I ever owned was already old, I changed the oil myself and dumped it down a sewer drain near our house in Hoboken, New Jersey. Got out from under that '63 Chevy Impala Super Sport with an old refrigerator tray filled with five inky black quarts of oil and poured it all right into the grate on the corner, just as I had seen others do it. Didn't think twice about the oil making its way through the sewers to the Hudson River, just a few blocks away. Didn't think about it at all back then.

But I've thought about it lots in the nearly forty years since. It still makes me wince. My wife and I started to recycle before anyone else we knew, taking bottles down to an Owens Corning glass plant a few miles from our apartment and waiting in line, along with a huge dump truck filled with glass, to weigh the two or three boxes of bottles we had in our trunk. I plant trees every year and water with a drip hose. I commute by train or bus, and walk wherever I can. I reuse paper towels.

So how could I have dumped used motor oil down a storm drain, not once but repeatedly? Simple. I wasn't aware that there

---

[1] Loosely adapted from "All Together Now," *Notre Dame Magazine,* Autumn 2008.

was anything wrong with what I was doing until a neighbor told me I shouldn't. As soon as he explained about the river, I realized he was right. I couldn't undo what I'd done. Now, nearly three decades later, every time I see a sewer grate embossed with the warning "Dump No Hazards—Flows Directly to River" with that generic outline of a fish next to it just to hammer the point across, I want to punch myself.

I was dumping oil just about a year before the first Earth Day in 1970. Most Americans who are alive today were born after that initial celebration of our planet. They are keenly aware of the natural world around them in large measure because they have been that way all their lives. Unlike me, they never knew a world where it was acceptable (in certain circles anyway) to use storm drains as dumps; where trash was routinely tossed out of moving cars (not me, but I saw plenty); where industry routinely discharged pollution into rivers and streams; and where curbside pickup referred not to recycling but to how you got White Castle hamburgers.

The intimate way we now know the natural world results from a series of environmental achievements in the decades after that first Earth Day. For most Americans today, a place like Love Canal—the notorious toxic dump that the Environmental Protection Agency declared clean a few years ago—signifies a hard-fought victory of public will. For them, the Clean Water Act is a fact of life that bans pollution. For them, living without the Clear Air Act regulations would be a smoggy step backward.

Each of these milestones was accomplished through tough legal and political battles. That is environmental history. Most people today no longer see environmentalism as a conflict, engaged in courtrooms or on angry marches. For the most part, the big environmental confrontations about pollution have already been fought. The important legislation is in place. Regulations are already on the books.

Continued improvement from this point on will be, by its very nature, incremental—a low-intensity war of long duration filled with incidental skirmishes. By contrast to the dynamic action of an earlier era, this could be seen as dull. *Erin Brockovich* and *A Civil Action* have been replaced by the pedestrian reality of enforcing existing laws and recording violations. Environmental protection, won with the legal equivalent of cannons, now will be advanced with slingshots and rulers.

That's not to say all the passion has been drained out of the environmental movement. It has taken something as dramatic as global warming to quicken the pulse of committed environmentalists, even if the problem is so complex that no single action or decisive blow can temper it. Recognizing the threat was just the first step. Convincing Americans—and their elected representatives—to sacrifice now in order to stave off a climactic cataclysm clearly will take more than it did to shame a naïve teenager in Hoboken to properly dispose of fouled motor oil. Warnings of rising seas and the dangers of carbon dioxide emissions couldn't kill sales of the huge Hummer. It took $4 a gallon gas to do that, and that lasted only a short time.

For the last few years, an insiders' debate has raged over the concept that environmentalism is dead.[2] The argument goes something like this: With so many victories secure, and ennui settling in, the old coalitions committed to cleaning up the natural and built environments have dissolved. Nothing of substance has taken their place. This may be an exaggeration, but it has been clear for some time now that environmentalism has been fundamentally transformed. Collaboration has replaced confrontation; conservation has supplanted regulation.

Big corporations, once considered adversaries, now are potential partners because they possess the technical know-how and the dollars to get things done right, especially when government is dragging its feet. The federal government once led the battle for the environment, but in recent years it has retreated. As a result, it has fallen to the states and local governments to patch together their own defense, such as the Northeastern states' Regional Greenhouse Gas Initiative, if only to try to shame Washington into taking bolder action.

---

[2] See Michael Shellenberger and Ted Nordhaus, "The Death of Environmentalism: Global Warming Politics in a Post-Environment World," (paper presented at the Environmental Grantmakers Association 2004 fall retreat, Kauai, Hawaii, October 2-6, 2004).

Where passion once was motivation enough, gimmickry and marketing recently have been used to convince people to save the environment, especially when they think the environment has already been saved. Consumers have become the new environmental superheroes, saving forests by buying flooring approved by the Forestry Stewardship Council; saving energy by replacing serviceable refrigerators with new Energy Star products; saving fossil fuel by buying a hybrid, even though some—like the hybrid Lexus RX 400h—are so loaded with options that they get fewer miles per gallon than many cars with conventional engines. But such green guilt can be easily assuaged by buying credits that support a wind farm in Oregon. Clear conscience is possible even in an SUV.

Over the past decades environmental consciousness has shifted in a way that has brought us full circle. Before the first Earth Day there was little understanding that environmental problems existed. Now there's a misunderstanding that most of those problems have been resolved, all the major battles have been won and pollution has been outlawed. What's actually happened is that we have entered an environmental turning point.

"The 20th century was the era of environmental brawn," John Cronin told me in 2005 when I first interviewed him for the *New York Times* in his new position as executive director of the Beacon Institute for Rivers and Estuaries. "The 21st century must be the era of environmental brains."

We were on board *Trust*, his beloved 29-footer, heading over the calm waters of the Hudson River toward Pollopel Island and Bannerman's Castle, a forbidding, fascinating place that stands as testimony to the vision, and the folly, of an eccentric man who thought of the Hudson as a private plaything. "I've got special permission," John told me as we docked *Trust*. When I jumped ashore from the bobbing boat, I had to trust him.

I spent most of that day with John, clambering over the rocks and broken bricks of the ruins of Bannerman's dream. I was as impressed with John's knowledge of the history of the Island and how to get around the rocky outcropping as I was with his obvious dedication to the environment, and of course to the river. As we stood on the crumbling edge of what had once been the balcony to Bannerman's estate, we looked out over the river—the same river into which my used motor oil had once flowed—and out toward Storm King Mountain, and John recounted for me, in a few compact minutes, the history of the modern environmental movement.

On the way back to Beacon, as I pressed John for more details about his life and about the role he had played in the environmental movement as Riverkeeper for so many years, he surprised me. Shocked would be more like it. He basically shut me off, told me that all that stuff was old history. Oh, it had been exciting enough while he and Kennedy had been fighting those monumental battles. And it certainly had been important, even essential. But that's not where the environmental movement is today, John said. He asked me to look around the broad belly of the Hudson, a river that he had helped bring back from the dead. The fierce battles of the past had helped stop the worst industrial pollution, that much was certain. But the Clean Water Act hadn't stopped the river from being polluted. It just regulates and registers the wastes that are still dumped into the river. There are permits and limits for sure, he said, but most people aren't aware that pollution still is regularly discharged into the river.

There's that word again—awareness. That day on the river with John taught me an important lesson about how to view the environment. I was just starting out on the environment beat, and it was a lesson I was glad to have learned early on. I thought of how the federal government in 2004 had declared the infamous Love Canal in Niagara Falls to be clean and stripped its name off the Superfund list of the most polluted sites in America. When I flew up to see what was left of the Canal, what I saw was aligned with what John had told me about the Hudson. The tons of toxic chemicals that had made Love Canal a byword for corporate greed and government incompetence were still there, buried beneath a blotting layer of soil. Block after block was empty, stripped of all evidence that people had once lived, played, dreamed and awakened there. Their driveways were still etched into the grass. The people were gone, but the toxic mix of chemicals that had chased them out lay there still, just below the ground. "Clean" clearly hadn't meant the same thing to the Environmental Protection Agency as it did to me, or to most people.

The evolution of environmentalism in the 21st century has made Solomon-like compromises an almost unavoidable aspect of environmental protection. As understanding of contemporary issues grows, so does the complexity of resolving those disputes. The era of take-no-prisoners environmental crusades is waning. Now, solutions are complex. For example, conservationists realize they might have to allow sustainable forestry to remove trees from one tract of Adirondacks woods in order to raise the funds needed to preserve a larger, more pristine tract of land within the park. Tree huggers can become tree cutters without abandoning their principals or their goals. Who knew?

In a real sense, this pragmatic new environmentalism has led to a fundamental shift in thinking: In the past, protecting the environment meant deciding what we should not do, and then acting to prohibit those things as completely as possible. Now, more often than not, paving the way for a sustainable world means determining what we should do and how we should do it.

In 2009, we mark the 400th anniversary of Henry Hudson's first voyage up the river that would provide a lifeline for a young nation. In that role, the river would become so horribly polluted with industrial discharges that the sturgeon that once were so plentiful, roiling the river's surface, nearly disappeared.

Today, however, after decades of legal challenges and court decisions, the lower Hudson has been cleaned up substantially, and the fish are returning. The great threat to the river is no longer that the Hudson is polluted and unloved. Rather, it is the crush of too many people who would love to live close to the water's edge. Managing the river and understanding its natural cycles are the clear challenges now.

John Cronin understands the transformation better than most. When he left Riverkeeper in 2000, he sensed that it was time to rethink his approach to the environment. He turned away from courtroom battles and focused on the river itself.

He founded the Beacon Institute with a $50 million grant from New York State. Despite misgivings from a few environmental groups that still did not trust corporations, in 2007 he formed a collaborative partnership with IBM.

In a subsequent interview, John told me that he had convinced IBM to use its data-collecting expertise to help develop a real-time system for monitoring every aspect of the Hudson River's life. Underwater sensors will track schools of fish so that discharges of heated water from power plants are suspended until the fish have moved on. Monitors at the bottom of the river will track clouds of pollution as they move downstream. Remote-controlled submarine cameras can visually check out river conditions and relay signals to computers on land, creating a record about the health of the river that, like a person's own medical file, could trigger early intervention to keep small problems from becoming crises.

Since 2000, Cronin has probably spent more time thinking about the new environmentalism than he has spent aboard *Trust*. He says he became aware that a transforming change was taking place the day he went to talk with an executive at IBM headquarters. He told me that after the interview ended, he looked out at the company's parking lot and saw car after fuel-efficient car with kayaks or canoes lashed to their roofs. The executive told him the vehicles belonged to company technicians and engineers, all born after the first Earth Day.

Those IBM employees probably never dumped motor oil down a storm grate. Many saw no trade-off between environmental sensitivity and working for a corporation—the two come together naturally for them. John said that in the old days of lawsuits and confrontation, all the talent and knowledge those young engineers possessed would have been off limits to the environmental movement.

That, he said, no longer makes sense because corporations have the money and the talent to get things done even when government can't or simply doesn't want to. Bringing both sides together is a matter of getting everyone to see things in the same way, or making them aware—as my neighbor in Hoboken did to me—of what was right.

"Can we really afford to turn them away? Do we even want to? I don't think so," John said. "There isn't room for permanent enemies anymore."

Since I spoke to John that day, I've come to see that he was right. More and more, we have turned to the car companies, and the appliance manufacturers, even city governments and public institutions, to make things more efficient so that we can protect the environment, and ourselves. It was necessary to go through the big battles and the drawing up of sides of past decades before we could reach this point. Now with trust, and a shared awareness of what needs to be done, it may be possible to take the next step. This is a lesson that John Cronin has already learned.

LEARNING THE RIVER

Susan Fox Rogers

The sight of a tug shoving or towing a barge delights me. Tugs appear small, and are usually painted a crisp red and white, or sometimes black and white. Set against the long heavy barges they move north and south against the current, in all weather, showing off their purpose, tenacity. It is hard not to use the word *cheerful*. The only time a tug isn't an endearing sight is when I am in my kayak, and the tug is pushing a barge straight for me.

I'm not sure why I didn't see the Virginia C as I crossed the river from Beacon to Plum Point. The river at this section is a little over a mile wide and the views north toward the Beacon-Newburgh Bridge then south into the Highlands spread into the distance. I'd been scanning the horizon, attentive to the movement on the river, because this was a section I had paddled only once before.

It was early in the season, the spring of 2006. I had decided this was the summer I would explore the length of the navigable river, drive north and south and put my boat in the water to see what I might see. The new landscapes would jolt me out of my comfortable, sad paddles in the reach off Tivoli, where I lived.

I was mourning my mother who had died in August. The river, I had found, gave me room to float about in my loss. I could let memories and images of her wash over me without fear of being pulled under. Whenever I began to drop into the depths of gloom something would happen—an osprey plummet in pursuit of a fish, or a cardinal flower appear ablaze on shore—to remind me of the wonder of life. I would take the next stroke and move on, thankful of that necessity.

John Cronin listened to my resolve to explore and suggested that I come paddle out of Beacon. "I'll help you get your boat in the water and come get you in Manitou." It was the sort of plan I could spend hours trying to orchestrate—a loop that involved fourteen miles south by water and then a quick return by car. The fact that John would be there beginning and end made it seem like he was traveling with me, though he had to work (and, at the time, he claimed he could never get his restless legs into a kayak; that has since changed). Still, I had to force myself out the door to drive one hour south. Venturing out of my reach felt a bit dangerous.

So there I was in my wetsuit—armor against the cold water below me. And there was the barge, looming out of the south, its rusted grey-red hull riding high in the water, a wall of steel nearly indistinguishable in color from that of the rusty-green water. The snout of the tug, painted a vibrant red, peeked above the barge from behind. All of this, impossibly near my port side. It is difficult to gauge speed and distance on water. And it's also hard to tell if a boat is heading right toward you or not. But from my water-level view there was no question the barge was bearing down on me. I knew this because it was close, not more than two hundred yards away. *A barge can't stop and it can't swerve.* It was up to me to stay out of the way either by sprinting toward land, hoping to squirt past or veer sharply south, keeping to the middle of the river until it surged by. I chose the later.

To ride down the middle of the Hudson where it is wide, where there's plenty of boat traffic and you are small and slow moving, this is to feel exposed. Clutching my paddle more firmly than I needed, I continued south. Within moments the barge and tug passed, the force of their deep speed grazing my right shoulder. The captain of the tug stood on deck and as he passed I thought I saw him shake his head before stepping into the cabin. I imagine he was relieved, but mostly irritated. I felt foolish. I should have seen the barge, but the sun high in the sky, the color of the boat and that of the water had all worked against me. The steady waves from the wake of the barge rocked my kayak. Once I caught my breath, I darted for shore.

I limped out of my boat on Plum Point. A gaggle of men had their fishing poles stuck in the water; I envied them their seeming casual sense of time. No one greeted me celebrating that I had made it. Or maybe I had an exaggerated sense of danger. I looked back at the eastern shore, where I had launched but a half hour ago. It had taken me a while to load all of my gear, which included extra clothes and enough food for a week. By mid-summer I would be heading out, hatches empty except for a jug of water. Vigilance would give over to the casualness of hot air and warm water. For now, though, I was ready for anything. Except my own stupidity.

I pulled out my cell phone. "I almost got run over by a barge," I reported without saying hello. A beat of silence.

"Boats do collide," John said.

I had spent the past five years paddling the river but in the last six months, since meeting John, my knowledge about the river had expanded and my view of it had changed. I had a lot more facts to work with—the Bay I crossed when I first launched from Beacon was called Biscuit Bay for the Nabisco factory that is now the Dia Art Museum. I saw that swimming across the river was one of my more careless adventures (though I'll never regret doing it). I knew about crabs and commercial fishing thanks to John's stories. And I knew, not only from his example, but from how he spoke of the river that it was not a playground. I had come to appreciate that the river is a working river, and that means stuff moving around—oil, or junked cars. John did not have a lot of patience for boaters and swimmers who did not respect the rules of navigation (you do *not* have the right of way!) but also the inexorable laws of tide and cold water. Above all, I now knew how little I knew, how five years on a river is just enough time to become acquainted. This river time didn't discourage me, it only made me want to learn more. I read, I paddled and wrote about what I saw, and I spent as much time tagging around with John as I could. I had never met anyone so generous with what he knew.

I stroked south, looking toward Pollepel Island, which is often mis-named Bannerman's for the Scottish (mad) man who built his castle on the Island. To the West lurked Storm King, and on the east Breakneck ridge. They both offer a dramatic drop, the river slithering by amidst wildness and green. This view makes people use words like *majestic* and *mighty*, two words I would like to ban in relation to this river. The Hudson may indeed be majestic but that one word flattens the complexity that I had come to know, the rich intertwining of beautiful and ugly that made me want to know the river. Though it looked like I was paddling through a picture postcard, the spring-muddy water lent a different story. The river felt broad and secretive, perhaps a bit worn.

From my perspective the river ended just past Pollopel, came to a gentle horseshoe curve and stopped, forming a large lake. From the south, the bend in the river also gives a sense that the river ends, so it's no wonder that sailors first journeying up the river named this point World's End. I continued south, and as I rounded Storm King I felt on edge, unsure what to expect as the currents picked up in exciting ways, the water agitated as if I might be spit out into the narrow passage of the river.

If the river has a symbol or mascot it is Storm King Mountain. I'd like to think of it as special for the long battle waged on its summit between Con Edison and commercial fishermen who joined hands with local environmentalists. Truth is, Storm King is an ordinary mountain. It's a rounded hump with exposed granite on the south side. Near those cliffs circled a kettle of turkey vultures, wings spread in a V, fingers splayed wide. They dipped around and around as if smelling their next stinky meal. The river *worn*? Storm King *ordinary*? These un-pious thoughts had roamed my mind since I had begun paddling the river; I never dared voice them. And then I met John.

I remember the first time John and I shared a dinner, or supper, as he says. We talked about John Steinbeck, Thomas Merton, and the river all in one breath. Land and spirit and place. Awe and irreverence intertwined. We laughed a lot. It's hard to cover so much in subject or tone in one dinner, but we did; I had met a mind with the sort of range that delights me. I knew I had found a friend. Despite a deep moral sense of the world—his notions of right and wrong, the value of a promise and hard work unshakable—John is utterly unsentimental about the river. *River shmiver*, he exclaimed during one of our conversations, sending me into gales of laughter. He is the environmentalist who has never hugged a tree. Didn't believe in hugging trees. And though I do hug trees, I found relief in John's perspective. I wandered around for days chuckling and repeating *river shmiver.*

In my sight sat the northern section of West Point. Young men jogged by on shore without looking out to wave; on a wide green field, cadets played soccer. The place looked peaceful, like a big summer camp. Once past World's End the real West Point emerges. The main building looks like a medieval castle and does not in any way match the modern buildings to the north. The building stands high above the water, as if perched on the side of a cliff, and below a narrow strip of land leads to a dock.

The land north of Con Hook is perhaps the prettiest I have seen anywhere. Sandy soil supports pine trees seemingly pressed flat by the wind. Rocks emerge from the sand, and I felt as if I knew this piece of land, though I'd never seen it before. I soon realized that it reminded me of the Indiana Dunes, where as a child I had spent my summers with my grandparents. In an instant, I felt the kiss of a breeze from the summer of 1971, when I was young and free and my family was whole. This return to childhood brought with it as well the hope of childhood. Then, life is about the future, looking to what will come next, what you will be "when you grow up." I savored that taste of hope as the current shoved me south.

I called John to let him know I wasn't far from Manitou. "It's beautiful out here. You shouldn't be in the office." No one should be in an office. I had tried office life for a few years when I lived in Manhattan. But it soon felt false, constraining. As a kid I never said, "I want to be a teacher," but that is what I have become. Teaching is in my blood—four generations back we all are teachers. But what drew me to the profession is the freedom it offers. What I did know as a kid was that I would need fresh air and movement to know myself and the world.

When John was a kid did he ever say that he wanted to be a lawyer, doctor, or firefighter, those careers we are fed by adults eager to secure the future? I doubt it. It must be hard to grow up into a career that does not exist. In some ways, what he is remains without easy definition. He occupies a unique territory that mixes activist, teacher, and environmentalist. Maybe he's still trying to figure out what he wants to be when he grows up. I realized that a lot of John's optimism (which is wildly contagious) comes from this fact: he is not set, that he is still looking for what is next. Like a kid full of hope, the future, not the past, is where John lives. I wondered what he might be looking forward to, what he might yet become.

I scooted toward a green buoy to cross the river before realizing that an enormous barge was right behind me, chugging south. I had never seen anything so wide on the river before, three barges lined up together. Three barges wouldn't fit on my reach off Tivoli and I realized how much wider and deeper, how much noisier and busier the river was here. I waited for the barges to pass then I crossed the river and swung into Mystery Point. I once visited the large house that stands at the point when the owner was renovating it to be a bed and breakfast. All of the bathrooms were done in marble with double showerheads. Scenic Hudson bought the surrounding land and house, and then turned it over to Outward Bound to use as their main headquarters. I wonder still what they did with those fancy bathrooms.

Just south I landed on a spit at the tip of Manitou, which to the Algonquian tribes meant Great Spirit. I stood and stretched, tired after four hours of movement and sunshine. Within minutes John was there, full of energy. I admired how he could go from looking like a river rat to put together in his nice suits and foreign-made ties. He cleaned up well, as we said in Central Pennsylvania. But I sensed on this day that he would have traded in all of those ties to be out on the river.

While I organized gear, John wandered the narrow beach, distracted but focused at once. I looked over to see why he wasn't helping me with my gear and saw that he had come to a rest, as if he'd found what he was looking for. He stood with his back to a tree and lined up with a boxy white house on the far shore. He extended his arms, fingers spread emphatically. I had no idea what he was pointing toward or looking at. At three in the afternoon, the sun hung high in the sky, flattening the water before me. Behind us, just twenty yards away raced the train tracks. South of us stretched the dozen houses of Manitou that cling to the water's edge.

"If you ever land here at high tide, line up with that house and this tree and you'll miss the rocks."

"Ok," I said with little conviction. I hadn't spoken to anyone in hours and I'd slipped into a reverie. "What's the story with that house?" I gestured toward the nearest house. Three stories high, the plywood weathering black in the sun, it looked both clumsy and desolate.

"See, if you line up you'll miss the rocks on either side." If I followed John's arm-directed trajectory I would land between rock outcroppings, visible then at low tide, and onto the sandy shore. That was where my kayak rested. "At high tide, you won't see those rocks."

"Right." But what he was suggesting was absurd. It had taken me years to learn the details of tree limbs and rocks in my reach off Tivoli. The next time I paddled this section of the Hudson I would not remember how to line up for a scrape-free landing. To do so would require a memory so expansive I felt my mind bend.

When Mark Twain was learning the Mississippi as a steamboat pilot—a river about four times the length of the Hudson and eight times its navigable length—he marvels at the supernatural memory required. "Now, if my ears hear aright, I have not only to get the names of all the towns and islands and bends and so on, by heart, but I must even get up a warm personal acquaintanceship with every old snag and one-limbed cotton-wood and obscure wood pile that ornaments the banks of this river for twelve hundred miles; and more than that, I must actually know where these things are in the dark."[1] The problem for Twain is my own in that "my memory was never loaded with anything but blank cartridges." Twain was exaggerating; I am not. There was no way that, day or night, I would recall this landing.

I wished I knew the details of every landing along the Hudson from Albany to Manhattan. I wanted to know who had landed and what stories rested in the gravel that littered the shores. When I first began exploring the river, I believed it possible to

[1] Mark Twain, "Life on the Mississippi" in *Mississippi Writings*, (New York: Library of America, 1982), 270.

learn these tales. But the more I found out, the more there was to know, like those Russian dolls that keep emerging, one inside the other. In the endless details, the river was so far out of my grasp. *Learning a river is hard.* Maybe that alone was worth learning.

John took me down to his former house, a grey cape that looks like it belongs on Cape Cod. No one was home so we peered in the back window at the wide living area, the cabinets he built, and the refrigerator that had fallen over on him. It was clear that he was heartbroken by returning to this place where he had lived for seventeen years. Here was a real home, where he saw the water go by, where he knew people by their boats. He suddenly, after three years, missed it horribly. There were many reasons to move, all of them related to being a good father and husband. I admired him for this, being able to sacrifice for those he loves. And I thought he was nuts to have let it go. *He had a house on the banks of the Hudson.*

John took me a short ways down the train tracks to a piece of land that has remained undeveloped because there's no way to gain access. He used to take his daughter to this small quiet cove when she was a child and they would swim together. I imagined him a playful but cautious father, tossing his kid into the air, floating aimlessly for hours in this secret, rocky, shrub-strewn place. It felt like perpetual summer. I watched John's movements, free and confident, in this world that is his. I envied that. He settled on a rock and looked west. We sat for a while without speaking.

Back at his car, my kayak and gear loaded, I asked again, "What's the story with this house?" I still hadn't gotten an answer from him, and the house seemed like it might harbor good, nasty stories. But there's nothing sensational about its tale, one that involves the local zoning board. The owners claim it's but two stories high; it's clearly three. No one gave them a permit to build a three-story house so mid-construction they abandoned the project. It looks odd in a stretch of the river where every inch of river shoreline is prized, where people buy homes for $700,000 and then tear them down.

This ordinary story I *will* remember. I will also remember this ordinary day: the feel of the sun on my shoulders, the sweetness of the land near Con Hook, my panic in front of the Virginia C, and John's sense of both happiness and loss as he showed me the neat grey house where he used to live along the river there in Manitou.

ENVIRONMENTAL REGULATION: EVOLUTION THROUGH INNOVATION

Stephen J. Friedman

The movement to protect environmental values is unusual in that in large measure it is coming to maturity within a single lifetime. John Cronin's life as an environmental leader has spanned this period and his personal evolution in that role has matched the powerful changes that have taken place. His leadership flows not only from his own deep knowledge and considerable personal force, but also from his recognition of the need for a system of environmental regulation rooted increasingly in science.

In referring to the maturity of the environmental movement, I mean simply that those values have become incorporated into the worldview of a wide swath of American society as well as throughout the world. China, and India, as well as other less developed nations have accepted the importance of the fundamental values of clean air and water; the public interest in open green spaces and preserving wild natural spaces— although each country is groping toward a different balance point between those values and economic development. To be sure, there remains disagreement on the degree of threat posed by everything from global warming to the extinction of species. Yet the Obama Administration is committed to protecting environmental values and Congress at this writing seems likely to adopt cap-and-trade legislation. The evolution of mainstream thought toward environmental consciousness is clear and irreversible.

Moreover, events have broadened the base of the supporters

of some environmental goals in unexpected ways. For example, the geographical location of oil reserves and the prospective cost of petroleum products for transportation have created new bedfellows for the environmental movement. The location of large oil reserves in potentially unstable or hostile countries has given the need for alternative liquid or gaseous fuels a national security dimension that will only increase with time, energy demand, scarcity and cost. It is not in the interests of the United States to permit political events in a handful of countries to determine whether the economy of this country or, indeed, the world, will be permitted to expand at what would otherwise be its natural rate.

Despite these developments, a large part of the traditional environmental movement continues to exhibit some of the characteristics of an embattled minority. Science has been used in a most basic manner—as a risk assessment tool, primarily to identify the threats to human life and health from environmental degradation. Many environmentalists continue to rely on the precautionary principle as the primary basis for regulation. Many remain of the view that there is no economical way to take advantage of the huge coal deposits in the U.S. without environmental degradation. They oppose nuclear power because of the very real failure, thus far, to find an effective and safe method of storing spent fuel rods. The rapid development of the Brazilian, Russian, Indian and Chinese economies has created inexorable new pressures for energy growth, with special emphasis on coal-fired plants in China and nuclear power in other countries, and similar pressures are being felt in the U.S. Where does that leave the movement to limit climate change?

Although wind and solar power can make an important contribution, it seems unlikely that alternative sources of energy will, in the intermediate term, be sufficiently large to satisfy growing world energy needs and avert adverse effects on the environment. The use of coal and nuclear energy are unavoidable. Moreover, it is perfectly clear that the causes of the threat of climate change are international in scope and that no nation, or small group of nations, can meet them alone. The difficulty of this challenge is exacerbated by the absence of any effective, international enforcement mechanisms—international treaties are not self-executing and performance under the Kyoto Protocol does not suggest that a new treaty, even with the participation of and ratification by the United States, would achieve the necessary results. In short, simple opposition to coal-fired plants and nuclear power will not be effective, and even if it were effective in the United States, it would not be effective elsewhere.

The preferable course in the short and intermediate term would be for defenders of environmental values to cooperate in developing practical bio-fuels and in finding better methods, based on more intensive science and engineering, to reduce or sequester carbon emissions from petroleum and coal-based fuels and to store or reprocess nuclear fuel rods.[1] If successful, these improved methods would be available to nations throughout the world. If the environmental movement were to work together with energy companies and industry to find satisfactory solutions based on science and greater factual knowledge, that would truly represent a new stage in the environmental policy debate, and would give rise to new approaches to environmental regulation.

What, one might ask at this point, does all of this have to do with an appreciation of the leadership of John Cronin in the environmental movement—a man who has devoted the major portion of his life to a single river? It is that the evolution of John's focus on the Hudson River has incorporated the whole evolution of environmental regulation, from identification of threats to increased reliance on science for regulation in a manner that has global applicability. His initial focus as the Hudson Riverkeeper was on protecting a single river and estuary system from the effects of discharges from the operations of specific plants of specific companies; on cleaning up contaminated sites in the river; and on preventing further adverse effects on water and fish.

Today, as Director and Chief Executive Officer of the Beacon Institute for Rivers and Estuaries,[2] John has dedicated himself to an extraordinarily ambitious project to place sensors in the

---

[1] This approach would require finding a political mechanism to safeguard the resulting plutonium.

[2] The author serves on the board of the Institute.

Hudson River that will monitor physical, chemical and biological
events in the river on a real time basis. The sensors transmit
data to various centers for scientific analysis with the aid of
sophisticated software provided by IBM. The objective is to be
able to base regulatory actions on deep knowledge of what is
actually happening in the river and estuary system at all times.
Another element of the Institute's work will be to reappraise
the policy and legal framework of clean water regulation in
light of the availability of very precise data about the changing
characteristics of the river and the estuary system. The results
will not only inform the activities of regulators in other nations,
the sensors and analytical systems will be a prototype for river
and estuary systems all over the world. They will permit the
debate between regulators and industry to be based on a common
data base.

With this drive to marry science and policy-making, John
Cronin is leading regulation of rivers and estuaries into the
21st Century. His reliance on science and real-time data is a
harbinger of environmental regulation in the coming years.
The environmental movement needs to follow his example and
become deeply involved in understanding and explaining the
significance of science for policy-making.

Technology Confluence and Environmental Stewardship

Harry R. Kolar

There have been a number of technological advances and trends that present exciting new opportunities in the domain of environmental monitoring and management. Over the past few decades we have seen an explosion of data and information in nearly all aspects of our lives; much of this is due to the Internet and related technologies which have effectively decreased the acquisition and dissemination cost of data and information to a wide range of "consumers." In parallel, significant progress has been made in the development of sensors—breakthroughs in new technologies accompanied by substantial improvements in reducing the cost of devices, further fueling their proliferation in our world. A related dimension concerns distributed intelligence in computing systems. Our ability to perform fairly complex computing is not limited to larger platforms such as servers or supercomputers, rather, relatively sophisticated calculations can now be performed on smaller, embedded computational devices which may be far removed, both physically and architecturally, from traditional systems. These elements collectively provide the *cyberinfrastructure* of the next generation intelligent systems to help advance our understanding of complex ecosystems such as rivers and estuaries.

Environmental data is acquired from a number of sources ranging from *in situ* sensors (that measure a variety of physical, chemical, and biological parameters in the real world) to three-dimensional geospatial representations of land masses, benthic habitats, and artificial structures. The addition of layers of geophysical and meteorological data from satellites or syndicated data services further adds to the challenge of data management for environmental systems. Data are the *atomic* constituents of environmental systems and provide the foundation for understanding and discovery. Data are the facts, the objective truths of the system devoid of context. The disciplines of Information Science and Knowledge Management have provided for us a useful construct known as the information or knowledge hierarchy which often uses a pyramid to illustrate the relationship between data, information, knowledge, and wisdom; with data at the base and wisdom at the apex.[1, 2, 3, 4] There are variants of these paradigms (as well as no true consensus on definitions); however, for the purposes of this paper it is sufficient to simply note that the progression from data to wisdom is accomplished by successive enhancements of context and relationships (this is an admittedly pedestrian description). We may think of information as the first stage of analysis of data that includes relationships and context and involves some level of processing. Information has a purpose and a user and this is the level at which most current computer systems operate: our information technology (IT) nomenclature is accurate. Knowledge is more elusive and may be characterized as either explicit or tacit and is sometimes described as "actionable." Knowledge may be thought of as answering the question "how" contrasted with information as dealing with "who, what, where, when, and why" classes of inquiries. Knowledge may be considered as an organized or structured body of information which also has local community facets tied to concepts such as shared meaning, insight, and understanding and may also contain a temporal component to indicate currency and applicability to the domain. Wisdom joins all we know in terms of knowledge and adds even higher level complex attributes such as reflection, values, and judgment and tends to support a "futures view."

[1] Curiously, the earliest reference to this hierarchy, although incomplete, is attributed to T. S. Eliot and his pageant play "The Rock," published in 1934 (Faber and Faber).

[2] Harland Cleveland, "Information as Resource," *The Futurist*, 16 (1982): 34.

[3] Milan Zeleny, "Management Support Systems: Towards Integrated Knowledge Management," *Human Systems Management*, 7, no. 1 (1987): 59.

[4] Russel L. Ackoff, "From Data to Wisdom," *Journal of Applied Systems Analysis*, 16 (1989): 3.

The purpose for introducing this somewhat esoteric concept for the environmental domain is straightforward: the next generation systems for monitoring are today being designed with unprecedented levels of distributed intelligence. The proliferation of sensors provides an incredible opportunity to capture in real time more data of various types on a much larger and broader scale and finer granularity. Coupled with high volumes of other data such as remote sensing (e.g., satellites, etc.) and geospatial data, the complexity of the input data and its "fusion" is a daunting endeavor for a holistic environmental observatory and management system, yet it holds considerable promise for advancing these systems.

With the ultimate goal of increasing our knowledge of natural systems, observatory and management systems must incorporate new capabilities not only to collect and analyze data and information, but to do this at new levels using existing knowledge and ultimately produce new knowledge. The next generation systems will also integrate modeling and simulation data in an intelligent and operational manner. For example, should a particular estuary sensor detect a high concentration of nitrogen that deviates from a number of baseline (historical) conditions, what is the significance of the "event"? Traditional systems may create an alarm condition with some level of notification. The next generation intelligent cyberinfrastructure will analyze the conditions using the full information and knowledge domain at hand, draw conclusions, and make decisions in near real time. These decisions may involve checking a multitude of other sensors to analyze the contaminant plume in terms of origin and progression and to cross correlate weather and geospatial information as to possible recent heavy rainfall in an agricultural area known to be using fertilizers. If the nitrogen sensors normally record measurements every hour, tracking the plume may warrant selectively and autonomically increasing the sensor sampling rates dependent on location and flow values of a tributary. If fixed weather reporting stations are not recording rainfall at their locations or are not available, higher resolution weather modeling may be initiated to run precipitation models for localized areas based on the system's knowledge of the geography and recent meteorological data from external sources. Hydrological models may then also be applied to predict the movement of the plume to assess the possible impact on particular fish species and a relevant set of scientists would be notified of the event and the system's actions based on their interests and responsibilities. This is a simple example to illustrate the sophistication level at which our next generation systems will be able to function.

As data are the core of these systems, inaccurate data can wreak havoc, especially in complex intelligent systems that aim to make sense of large volumes of data with many parameters. The consequences can be wide-ranging: a research-focused system may simply derive incorrect conclusions concerning a hypothesis, but the implications for operational systems such as those connected with drinking water or flood control could be serious in terms of public health or safety. Even in the case of the former, the ramifications may extend to policy: consider the case of a "sensor drift" problem declared mid-February 2009 by the U.S. National Snow and Ice Data Center (NSIDC) that tracks arctic sea ice and uses this data for temperature change studies.[5] The satellite sensor problem produced inaccurate data that underestimated the amount of arctic ice by 500,000 square kilometers, an area larger than the State of California. The problem was identified over one month after the real-time data was collected and only when the NSIDC was contacted by "puzzled readers" who noticed discrepancies in the data. The NSIDC advised on their public website that four data sets were affected, the past six weeks of data should not be used, and that they were working to correct the problem.[6]

There are two salient points of this anecdote in the context

[5] Alex Morales, "Arctic Sea Ice Underestimated for Weeks Due to Faulty Sensor," *Bloomberg.com*, 20 February 2009, http://www.bloomberg.com/apps news?pid=20601110&sid=aIe9swv)qwIY (accessed June 3, 2009).

[6] National Snow and Ice Data Center, "New Data Products, Updates, and Other Data Announcement," http://nsidc.org/data/news.html, comment posted February 18, 2009 (accessed June 3, 2009).

of next generation distributed intelligent cyberinfrastructures: the first relates to the idea that sensors must continue to become "smarter" with some level of intelligence to automatically detect and alert us to problems and to prevent the introduction of "bad" data into the overall system. As seen by the NSIDC example, multiple data sets were affected and the problem was not resolved quickly (note that the sensor data is characterized as "near real time").[7] Not only is time and effort involved in correcting these situations, there is also a direct cost factor associated with communication costs for transmitting flawed data. Progress here is already being made with embedded intelligent sensor platforms and this has only been possible in recent years and will continue to improve over time. The ability to detect these types of problems as close to the data source is critical, as it is far more costly should dubious data enter the system. Identification of problems of this type is especially important for sensors that are remotely deployed and must function in harsh conditions such as aquatic installations subject to corrosion and biofouling.[8] The second point involves a more holistic view of a real-time intelligent system's capabilities. As mentioned earlier, the advances we hope to gain from these advanced systems are due not only to increasing numbers of real-time sensors in an ecosystem such as an estuary, but the ability to obtain new knowledge from the system using new analytical techniques which work with many different data and information sources. This speaks to the relationships of parameters within the entire complex natural system: some relationships may be very complex and/or may be subtle, detectable only by advanced computer algorithms. The integrity of the system is then highly dependent on the quality of the data and it is imperative to have some consistent measure of this quality.

It should be noted that standard data quality checks are performed routinely by organizations such as the NSIDC and the sensor drift problem would have eventually been detected

---

[7] At the time of this writing, over one month later, no further information was available regarding the sensor data sets.

[8] Biofouling refers to the undesirable surface accumulation of various organisms in an aquatic environment resulting in the impaired operations of equipment.

and corrected; in this particular case the erroneous data did not affect the findings regarding arctic ice trends. For environmental observatory and management systems with significant investments in real-time technologies, these problems can compromise their efficacy and, at a minimum, introduce unwanted latencies in these systems, which could adversely affect early warning subsystems.

Combined progress in several key technologies has brought us to a point in time for which environmental system proponents have been eagerly waiting. The dreams of leaders in this field are driven by their passions for improving our knowledge of important and complex ecosystems to better manage and protect these precious environments globally. Environmental scientists and environmentalists alike appreciate the complex interrelationships of the various natural subsystems and that our understanding will only be improved with new technologies to capture accurate and timely data and to ultimately transform them into knowledge. This is now attainable through the evolution of a number of technologies that are able to collaboratively act. The topmost level of the knowledge pyramid hierarchy is that of wisdom and to date this has not been demonstrated in any meaningful way through technology—for now, wisdom remains with our environmental stewardship visionaries who not only desire to gain new knowledge through the development and application of innovative technologies, but actively apply this newfound knowledge to policy and education at the global scale. A quote from Ralph Waldo Emerson embodies the spirit and aspirations of these pioneers: *Do not go where the path may lead, go instead where there is no path and leave a trail.*

LARGE THOUGHTS ABOUT A SMALL ISLAND

Mary G. Burns

For thirteen years I had agonized over the fate of one of the smallest islands in the huge Hudson River: Magdalen Island. Over the years, looters had dug randomly, destroying the archaeological record on the chance of finding an arrowhead. Trying to protect the core of its eight acres from the illegal diggers seemed a hopeless challenge when its owners—the State of New York—didn't seem to have the resources or the concern that were needed; yet trying to publicize its plight risked attracting more artifact hunters. What to do?

I had grown so fond of the puffy bit of trees jutting up out of the vast expanse of water that I took to calling it, endearingly, "my puffball." Consisting of mostly graywacke / sandstones, this rocky little gem sits approximately a half-mile from the west bank of the town of Red Hook. It is easy to reach by boat, but far enough away for illicit activities to take place with no one watching. In my many trips to the island, I had never encountered anyone in the act of digging, although looting continued.

My first introduction to Magdalen was while pursuing a Masters degree in Environmental Studies at Bard College. I was determined to study it to see if any undisturbed soil remained amongst the more than 200 looter holes. In addition, I wanted to see if protections could be put in place. I was proud to be following distantly in the footsteps of Dr. Mary Butler who in 1939, and 1940 with a grant from the Carnegie Corporation, surveyed some forty archaeological sites in the Hudson Valley, including Magdalen, then known as Goat Island. (I love that name and that is how I have referred to the island ever since.)

Even at that time, Dr. Butler remarked in her field notes that the island already showed evidence of looting. She determined that it had been a seasonal campsite, and from the substantial amount of chert flakes, had probably been a tool-making workshop as well.

But not all was lost. From a modest amount of archaeological testing I carried out in 1995 with the assistance of Dr. Christopher Lindner of Bard College and the late New York State Archaeologist Robert Funk, it was clear there was more to be learned. Tiny remains such as a burned fish bone and charred nuts and seeds were there to tell us of the subsistence strategies of these early Native campers. Consider that in archaeology, history is a book where layers of residue form the pages of chapters; careless, unrecorded digging tears the pages from the book and scatters them so that the history is lost.

Over the years since getting my degree and with permission of the New York State Department of Environmental Conservation, I have tried many techniques to save the site, short of a full-scale excavation that would be prohibitively expensive and difficult in terms of getting people and supplies to the island every day for the many field seasons it would take. I've attempted a stabilization strategy protecting a pit from further digging with soil and buried chain link fencing; I brought a ground-penetrating-radar crew to the island to see if that technology would tell us more about what is in the soil; with a colleague's technical expertise, I created for the state a GIS map of the campsite's looter holes; I faithfully replaced the State's "Don't Dig" signs when they were vandalized; I was dedicated—okay, obsessed—but I was a frail reed against a wind of unlawful avarice.

Although I've shown the island and my work there to more than fifty newcomers, many of them volunteers without whom I could not have achieved my goals, still I have done much of the work alone. Indeed I think it is the sheer joy of being alone—during more than sixty solo trips—on the Hudson that has provided the sustaining power behind my work. But who wouldn't want to work alone on a beautiful little island with a view of the Catskill Mountains, marshes, and the wide expanse of the powerful Hudson? And canoeing to work every day...well, you just can't beat that!

To get to Goat, I unload my canoe at the foot of Tivoli near the railroad tracks. If an Amtrak train whizzes by, I heartily wave to the conductor and she/he blows her/his horn and I think it's a friendly "bon voyage" just for me, not a warning for cars and pedestrians at the Tivoli railroad crossing. Buoyed by the send-off, I carefully pack the canoe with supplies, because I know it is futile to accomplish anything, and it's a schlep to canoe all the way back to civilization if I forget one single thing: notes and notebooks, camera, map that I'm working on, Excel spreadsheets with data, pencils, measuring tapes, flag tape, Sharpies, drinking water, a snack. Have I forgotten something? I use a one-person, very tipsy canoe and everything must be kept dry so I use a dry-bag as well as a multi-layer trash bag for the supplies. Some of my trips have been quite hair-raising. A particularly unpleasant combination is when dealing with wind blowing one way, current going another way, white caps, and passing large freighters that produce huge waves as they make their way up or downriver. Other days, it is calm, peaceful with just the plops of my paddle and birds calling that break the silence.

Once on the island, I set to work mapping, taking measurements and notes, and lose myself in the project. It is quiet, just me rustling a few leaves as I walk between looter pits. Then, out of nowhere, I hear a crash or a very loud rustle that is not of my own making and I am suddenly panicked. Am I safe? Is it a looter? What will I do or say? This is the part I hate...or is it? I have always said I would like to confront whoever is doing these bad deeds. Try to educate them about the importance of saving archaeological sites on state land for future generations when archaeological methods will be so improved by advanced technologies that archaeologists will be "looking" into the earth to see the layers of artifacts that inform the history of a site instead of excavating which is, in itself, destructive. Still, my heart races. "Hello," I call out as something/someone comes near. If it's a person, chances are they have seen my canoe and expect someone to be on the island, but I have no idea who/what is approaching. In a grove of saplings, seedlings, bushes, and tall trees—all in leaf—I cannot see more than five feet in front of me. Sometimes it is a person and other times a squirrel or opossum;

amazingly, both seem to rustle the leaves the same way.

On September 13, 2007, the rustling leaves that broke my reverie turned out to be my new friend Susie Rogers bringing her friend John Cronin to the island. They kayaked across the bay, came up the steep bank from a landing spot, and on first seeing the pock-marked area, John said to me, "More New Yorkers have to know about this." I knew John by reputation, and was surprised that his passion could extend beyond the natural resources of the Hudson to this, a cultural resource—never the site of construction, just a seasonal campsite for unnamed tribal groups for millennia before the Europeans arrived.

That's the kind of guy John is: he thinks broadly, holistically, globally. "This," he said, "is the poster child for all the damage being done to archaeological sites, not only along the Hudson, but all over New York." For me, this immediate reaction tipped the balance toward making Goat Island a cause rather than a secret.

Being an activist with a broad network of friends and contacts, John asked if he could present this story to his friend, Anthony DePalma of the *New York Times*. He felt that the only way to halt the looting would be to make people aware of the loss and the illegality, and perhaps cause the state to pay attention and even strengthen its laws.

So, on a very cold December 5th in 2007, you would have seen me paddling toward the island with Anthony DePalma and his photographer carting thousands of dollars worth of camera equipment. Nearing Goat, we had to break ice to keep paddling, and when we were at the site, snowflakes began flying. A week later, a large article appeared in the Metro Section of the *Times*, and my standing with the state officials changed. Merlin, John Cronin, had waved his wand and I possessed credibility to go along with my knowledge and passion.

I cannot say that much has changed for "my puffball," but we'll see as the seasons progress and I continue to monitor, and the state environmental officers respond to my calls. The miscreants have to be locals who can get to the island quickly by boat, carrying tools that casual picnickers wouldn't have. Catch one or two of them and the situation could change. The situation could change even more if word went out through the collecting community—and there is such a community, trading on eBay—that enforcement was up, and that fines and confiscations were increased. These changes will come about through legislation, and John is leading me through an effort to make even a dysfunctional legislature function for the public and scientific good.

But one thing has changed. In the fall of 2008, I, along with Hudson River Heritage, nominated the island to be one of the Preservation League of New York State's *Seven to Save* Endangered Properties of 2009 and it became the first archaeological site ever to make the list. In this Quadricentennial year of Henry Hudson's jaunt up the river, it is appropriate for the island to receive this recognition; Hudson would have seen and perhaps even set foot on the island. The League's attention will raise awareness of the fragility of archaeological sites on state land.

Some day I would like to know enough to walk John back through the millennia of life as lived at the campsite on Goat Island, what fish were taken from the river, what birds were netted, what plants grew there and how they were used. That is a history we have yet to uncover. Until that day, I will say "Thank you for giving me my voice, John, and thank you for missions yet to be accomplished."

A River Beckons Home

Alexandra Dapolito Dunn

"But I go with my friend to the shore of our little river, and with one stroke of the paddle, I leave the village politics and personalities, yes, and the world of villages and personalities behind, and pass into a delicate realm of sunset and moonlight..."
"Nature," Ralph Waldo Emerson (1844)

Ralph Waldo Emerson was bewitched by nature and in particular, rivers and the magic and order of the hydrologic cycle. As I reflect upon my relationship with the Hudson River for this essay, I realize I understand his captivation. My earliest memories of the Hudson River are those of my child eyes peering out the window of my parents' green 1959 Chevrolet Bel Air with whitewall tires, as we drove many a weekend across the Tappan Zee Bridge from Valley Cottage, New York to visit my grandparents in the Bronx. It was the early 1970s, and from my relatively unconstrained position in the back seat (as compared to my own children today), I would look out across the river's grey water and let my gaze rest on the Castle in Tarrytown. I imagined the magical life of the royals inside, their joyful music, and the princesses' colorful gowns. The river spanned so far each way it could have been an ocean. I was too young to realize during these drives, which later continued after the passage of the Bel Air via a red 1970 Chevrolet Chevelle Malibu, that the Hudson was subtly weaving its own magic, searing into my subconscious a connection to it and even a promise to bring me friends and comfort. This connection and promise, however, would lay dormant for nearly three decades.

My later childhood years gave me wonderful opportunities to connect with other distinct bodies of water—a Great Lake and another great river. In 1977 we moved to Glencoe, Illinois, on

Chicago's North Shore and the spectacular Lake Michigan. This Lake has certainly captured the imagination and inspired many, particularly Pulitzer prize winning poet and Chicago resident for a time Carl Sandburg. Sandburg beautifully describes in his poem *The Harbor* Chicago's "blue burst of lake" and its "[l]ong lake waves breaking under the sun, [o]n a spray-flung curve of shore."

The midwest, however, did not keep its hold on my family, and college on the East Coast led me to Harrisonburg, Virginia— proximate to the lazy Shenandoah River. Referenced by John Denver in *Take Me Home, Country Roads*, this river was indeed a source of inspiration. I camped by its shores and slipped along its muddy banks, even floating on it in an anchored lawn chair, a bobbing cooler of refreshments on a short line.

A call to pursue environmental law led me after college to the political mecca of Washington, D.C. There I came to befriend the rocky and turbulent Potomac River, and its uniquely different Maryland and Virginia sides. Walt Whitman wrote prose referring to the "city of the wide Potomac, the queenly river, lined with softest, greenest hills and uplands" and in his poem *By Broad Potomac's Shores* he describes "Virginia's summer sky, pellucid blue and silver" and "the forenoon purple of the hills."[1] Law school study breaks were spent hiking along its banks with my boyfriend on Maryland's Billy Goat Trail. When that boyfriend became a fiancé years later, we took our engagement photographs in jeans overlooking the Potomac River Gorge in Virginia's Great Falls Park. When that fiancé became a husband, we later strolled with our two children to spot deer along the Potomac's verdant banks near our home in Potomac Falls, Virginia. As my work as an environmental attorney progressed, I cultivated a specialty in clean water law, and soon found myself navigating D.C.'s infamous rush hour in a hybrid vehicle bearing a *Treasure the Chesapeake* vanity tag of *H2OESQ* – water lawyer.

My legal cases focused on the most detailed nuances of the federal Clean Water Act (CWA). One case, *National Ass'n of*

1 Walt Whitman, "By Broad Potomac's Shore" in *Leaves of Grass: Noon to Starry Night* (1891-92).

Home Builders v. Defenders of Wildlife, 549 U.S. 1105 (2007), concerned whether the United States Environmental Protection Agency (EPA) improperly delegated the CWA's permitting program to the State of Arizona—the Supreme Court held that EPA did not. Another concerned whether the South Florida Water Management District's pumping of stormwater in the Everglades required permits—the Supreme Court held maybe (the battle still rages today) (*South Florida Water Management District v. Miccosukee Tribe of Indians*, 541 U.S. 95 (2004)). A third concerned a multi-year battle over whether the District of Columbia could express total maximum daily loads for key pollutants of concern in an annual or seasonal manner—the United States Court of Appeals for the District of Columbia Circuit held that it could not (*Friends of the Earth v. EPA*, 446 F.3d 140 (D.C. Cir. 2006)). A fourth evaluated whether EPA regional guidance documents being used as regulation in the field could be reviewed as final agency action—the United States District Court for the District of Columbia held that they could not (*Pennsylvania Municipal Authorities Ass'n v. Horinko*, 292 F. Supp.2d (D.D.C. 2003)). A final example looked at whether EPA properly approved West Virginia's antidegradation implementation procedures—the United States District Court for the Southern District of West Virginia held that some were properly approved, others were not (*Ohio Valley Environmental Coalition v. Horinko*, 279 F. Supp.2d 732 (S.D.W.Va. 2003)). This work was gratifying and exciting. I was shaping the nation's clean water future, parcing challenging issues accompanied by sharp-minded lawyers from all over the nation. The only application of my legal training and practice I thought I could enjoy more was one in which my responsibility would be to instill in a future generation a passion for clean water and a love of the law. Opportunity then knocked. In summer 2007, the chance to come to Pace Law School and become the Assistant Dean of its top ranked Environmental Law Program was mine. We left D.C. and here is where the Hudson River reenters this story.

With only one weekend to find a house, I instinctively narrowed our search to the Hudson River towns. I knew if we were going to live in New York, we had to be by the Hudson. I now believe this sense of direction, a sense of wanting to be by the river, came both from the deep recesses of my mind—recalling those trips across the river as a young child—and my lifetime connections with various water bodies. Although I hadn't seen the river since 1977, something about being near it was as easy and comfortable as talking to an old friend after the passage of many years. The river felt like home. The river could ground and root us.

And so, we trekked in and out of homes along the river, and settled on a humble home in Croton-on-Hudson. Our new town is defined by the river, both in name and in geography. The Croton and Hudson Rivers meet to form Croton-on-Hudson's boundaries to the south, east and west. Croton-on-Hudson's topography includes low lying areas along the Hudson River, the Croton River Gorge, and a plateau to the north which reaches an elevation of 600 feet within only a mile of the Hudson River.

The Hudson River then began to deliver on its long ago promise to be something special in my life. Each morning, as I round the bend on Route 9 south, I am snapped out of my morning mental reverie as I glance to the right to see an ever-changing spectacular river show. Sometimes it is grey and nearly invisible; for months frozen solid; other times churned up and wavy with ocean worthy whitecaps. The river can be midnight blue and smooth as glass, with hardly a ripple; and on my favorite days, the sun high in the sky overlooks an azure blue river dotted with white-sailed boats, as enchanting as a carnival. When the moon is full, its reflection glances off the water while a multitude of stars blink in the sky. The Tappan Zee's green lights twinkle just off in the distance, reminding me of my childhood traverses. It is a bewitching sight.

I have the opportunity to teach dynamic and passionate students, and to work with a team of dedicated Hudson River enthusiasts at Pace Law School. My course in Environmental Justice draws students who are concerned about equity in society and providing effective vehicles for marginalized members of society to make themselves heard. We discuss the absolute importance of public participation in environmental decision making and the need for transparency and accessibility in environmental information, particularly technical and scientific information. Our class uses the Hudson River as a living classroom. In Fall 2008, my students and I met with community activists from Yonkers on a rainy Saturday morning at the Beczak Environmental Education Center on the Hudson riverfront. We learned that without this Center and its engaging programs, many low income and minority children in the community would have no contact with the river, and never have a chance to connect with this glorious resource. We then walked up the hill into the surrounding neighborhood, described as blighted and dead by advocates of a very large upscale retail and residential complex. What we found was a lower income neighborhood, where adults of many ethnicities were pushing children in strollers, buying fruit and groceries at open air produce stands, and drinking coffee and laughing by the street side. While this neighborhood was certainly not upscale, it was without question a vibrant, affordable area for many marginalized members of the Hudson River Valley population, who without training to advocate for their interests, would soon find themselves pushed out by gentrification. The students began brainstorming solutions almost immediately—how could affordable housing be preserved; how could a connection to the river be promoted; were there "win-win" solutions for this community—economic prosperity and affordable living near one of the world's largest cities? The morning was more eye-opening than the strongest cup of espresso could ever be.

In a similar wake-up moment, as part of a class research project, one of my students attended a Tappan Zee Project public information meeting on a weekday evening. She was struck by the lack of public transportation options to reach the meeting, that all written materials were in English, and that little opportunity was provided for the public attendees to participate in the discussions. She reported to our class that she found the meeting, as a source of information, generally inaccessible. This meeting, which was designed to engage the "public," presented engagement barriers to an educated English speaker, comfortable with high-level and detailed environmental information, and naturally at ease in a public meeting setting. This experience allows one to see easily how minority and low-income members of our community right here in the Hudson River Valley can become outsiders when environmental decisions impacting their lives and livelihoods are undertaken. By exposing my students to classroom dialogue and learning, complemented by hands-on field experience, I hope they will become the kind of future leaders who think broadly about the definition of community and take proactive steps to involve all members of society.

Not only does my classroom teaching draw on the Hudson, but also my own family life here is truly river-centric. My children, now six and nine, know the story of Storm King Mountain, told dramatically by me during rides exploring north. They have asked in stunned innocence why anyone would want to destroy a mountain. My daughter has camped with the Girl Scouts along the river in Croton Point Park, a former County landfill, today a beautiful park. We have ridden the Ferry-Go-Round from Tarrytown to Haverstraw and back, recalling how ferries were the primary mode of transportation across the river through the 1800s. Our family church and my children's school, St. Augustine, sits in Eagle Park, Ossining, on a bluff above the river. On Sunday mornings, we look out over the river as we pray for peace, health, and hope while church bells ring. We have learned that General George Washington and his troops are believed to have camped at Eagle Park, and that local historians suspect subterranean passages were built as possible escape routes for Washington's troops. We take the Hudson Line into the city, admiring the palisades, as the train almost floats on the river. We have spent lazy Saturday mornings trolling for beach glass along Croton Point's sandy shores. We even have dipped our toes in the water at Croton Point's beach, where many people splash and swim in the summer. And although not of perfect water quality by far, the Hudson is swimmable again.

In Summer 2008, I spent a week on the Sea Wolf R/V, a State University of New York at Stony Brook research vessel, with *River Summer*, traveling the Hudson from its mouth in the Long Island Sound to the Troy Dam near Albany. We then got into a van and drove further to observe one of the many tributary origins of the river north of Albany. A collaborative program of the Environmental Consortium of Hudson Valley Colleges and Universities, *River Summer* brings together Hudson River based faculty to share their knowledge, experiment with new ideas, and learn from one another while transiting up the Hudson River. Supported by The Andrew F. Mellon Foundation, and coordinated by scientists and experts at Columbia's Lamont-Doherty Earth Observatory, *River Summer* is a dramatic and unforgettable immersion into the science, history, and policy of the Hudson River. *River Summer* participants are drawn from faculty of diverse higher education institutions in the Hudson River Valley. Through life on the Sea Wolf and non-stop discussions among the participants, *River Summer* fosters learning and experiences which can change how we all teach our students. One sultry July afternoon, fanning ourselves on Sea Wolf's forward deck, we were mesmerized by fifteen bald eagles perched high in the trees along the river's banks. We trolled for sturgeon, and measured and counted these "living fossils," among the most ancient of fishes. Is the Hudson still as magical as it was when I looked at the Castle? Oh yes indeed. And, although far from fully healthy, it is fishable.

In my short time as an adult resident of the Hudson River Valley, I have come to realize that the river is more than just a geographic icon. The Valley is inspiring because of the people working here to ensure the river's history and health. I have had the privilege of meeting and being inspired by passionate river experts. Top among these inspirational Hudson River individuals is the subject of this collection, John Cronin. I met John within weeks of coming to Pace, and our mutual respect for the environment and its waters and concern for the Clean Water Act's future has led to many wonderful conversations. As I told John of my work in Washington on water issues, he quickly and emphatically told me of the CWA's many failures and its underutilized provisions. John cited the Congressional Purpose of the law "to restore and maintain the chemical, physical, and biological integrity of the Nation's waters" and the "policy of Congress that the President . . . take such action as may be necessary to insure that to the fullest extent possible all foreign countries shall take meaningful action for the prevention, reduction, and elimination of pollution in their waters . . ." 33 U.S.C. § 1251(a), (c). I am not sure I agree with John that Congress ever contemplated complete elimination of discharges of pollutants to U.S. waters, as the very statute which begins with such a lofty goal proceeds to create an extensive, state-delegated permitting program to authorize and control continued discharges. (*See* 33 U.S.C. § 1342(a)). Many of the cases I worked on in Washington focused on adding or removing sources from the scope of this very permitting program. The statute also addresses the allocation of "total maximum daily loads" of pollutants among dischargers (33 U.S.C. § 1313(d))—again recognizing continued, albeit controlled and reduced, pollutant presence. The CWA has been amended several times since its original passage, and none of the amendments focused on new programs or mandates to achieve a complete elimination of pollutants. As an example, a 1987 amendment added a needed program to manage, but not eliminate, stormwater. (*See* 33 U.S.C. § 1342(p)). Even EPA's 1990 combined sewer overflow policy, endorsed by a 2001 amendment (33. U.S.C. § 1342(q) (1)), anticipated residual overflows after massive infrastructure investment.

Despite the fact that the statute may fall short of John's desire, my work with city water and wastewater officials, and with the EPA, shed light on many tremendous successes due to the CWA, such as improved underground infrastructure, advanced treatment technologies, stormwater management, green infrastructure, and urban revitalization. However, I do concur with John in his assessment that provisions of the CWA loaded with potential and powerful language and important vision are underutilized. While John cites to the Congressional Purpose and Goals, I frequently look to provisions like the essentially dormant—but incredibly thoughtful—watershed-based Continuing Planning Process in 33 U.S.C. § 1288(b)). I absolutely believe that the statute is ill-suited to what is truly needed today—the management of water as a single resource. The statute by design separates clean water and drinking water management, segregates point and nonpoint sources, fails to promote water conservation and careful management of a strained and limited resource, and essentially does not facilitate a watershed approach to water. I support John's call for reform of the CWA and for a new paradigm that challenges all of us to strive for better water quality and water management—both in the United States and worldwide.

I feel fortunate to have had this opportunity to reflect on the Hudson River, my relationship to it, and the legal system in which I play a part. I am confident that the river and its dynamic leaders like John Cronin will inspire and motivate me for years to come. I am honored to be among a group of individuals who are not afraid to let their passion for the Hudson lead them. I am thankful that this particular river has led me home, and reflect how true to me ring Emerson's words in his 1827 poem *The River*:

> *"And I behold once more*
> *My old familiar haunts; here the blue river,*
> *The same blue wonder that my infant eye*
> *Admired. . ."*

Musings on the Future of Higher Education

Joseph M. Pastore, Jr.

Eventually, one learns there are moments in life that pose little meaning, except in retrospect. Sometimes those moments evolve in mutually exclusive ways to form a portrait greater than the sum of its parts.

One such moment was circa 1983 when, as Pace University's Vice President for Academic Affairs, I was called upon by the university's trustees to advance reasons why the university's School of Law should offer graduate study leading to an LL.M. degree in Environmental Law as opposed to programs perhaps more consistent with the university's historical repertoire, namely taxation or even international law. I made my case and, despite some trustee reticence spawned largely by uncertainty shrouding the innovative nature of the program, the LL.M. in Environmental Law was launched.

In the years that followed, I went on to become provost of the university and to address the multitude of issues that confronted a large, multi-campus institution determined to build an even greater standing in higher education. Occasionally, however, I would pause to measure and admire the Law School's waxing national and international environmental law reputation.

One such pause was for a Law School Commencement day in May 1994. The ceremony included awarding an honorary degree to John Cronin who, along with Professors Nicholas Robinson and Robert F. Kennedy, Jr., co-founded the Pace Environmental Litigation Clinic. I knew Nick as a longtime colleague and I knew Bobby Kennedy in a way the world knew him. But I didn't know John Cronin other than he was a prime mover in the work of Riverkeeper, an organization dedicated to improving and preserving the Hudson River ecosystem.

Flash-forward to 2008 when I was asked by Pace President Stephen Friedman to facilitate the formation of a University Center for Excellence on the Environment[1]—an effort to foster interdisciplinary and collaborative programming among the many environmentally related programs and activities within the University.

It was that assignment that introduced me to John and, in turn, prompted so many reasons why we should have connected much sooner. John grew up in Yonkers. I had come to know Yonkers fairly well given my U.S. District Court appointment as Monitor and Special Master in *United States v. Yonkers*, a desegregation case that I had overseen from 1986-2006. John and I would find reason to share reflections on the case. Also, John had studied and written on the ecological theology of Thomas Merton. I spent just over fifteen years as a student, faculty member, dean, and provost at Saint Bonaventure University—the institution where Merton taught and, as noted in his *Seven Storey Mountain* and other writings, was beckoned to begin his life as a Catholic priest—not with the Franciscans who founded St. Bonnie's, but with the Trappists at their abbey at Gethsemani in Kentucky.

Working with John Cronin and getting to know him, and the less than orthodox professional path he had taken, was not only helpful to my work, it caused me to elevate my thinking about the role formal education, especially higher education, plays in human development. Eavesdropping on John's life reminded me that, unlike some, I was fortunate to enter adult life at a time of reasonable peace and prosperity, along with those early "baby boomers" who embraced college with the same unquestioned commitment that we carried into a kindergarten classroom thirteen years earlier.

Those who know John Cronin know that unquestioned commitment, and thus the path commonly taken, has never been the case for John. John is both exceptional and an exception; his life and intellectual formation prompts me to wonder about

---

[1] Pace Academy for Applied Environmental Studies: A Pace University Center for Excellence.

assumptions and forces likely to influence the essence of higher education in the 21st Century—many of which are reflective of the path John has taken. Will, indeed should, the future of higher education cultivate more or fewer John Cronins?

SOMETHING IS HAPPENING

Something is happening. The world seems different. The feeling calls to mind the poetic power of Yeats' *Second Coming*[2] when he writes:

> *Things fall apart; the centre cannot hold;*
> *Mere anarchy is loosed upon the world,...*
> *The ceremony of innocence is drowned;...*

Perhaps such deep reflection is prompted by the quiet of the moment at which I pen these musings, a snowy New Year's Eve. But I think not. It is "noise," not quiet, that prompts such thoughts—"noise" that suggests we are at a palpable inflection point in world history, a point likely to change the "centre" as we have known it.

That the "centre" may not hold is not necessarily something to fear. Rather, it appears we may be at the precipice of a progressive era—one that is ours to lose. But, how is that evident and what might it mean for higher education? Three factors come to mind.

First, there is and will be no shortage of rhetoric predicting the historically symbolic impact the election of Barack Hussein Obama will have on the United States and, some say, the world. Yes, reason dictates we should reserve judgment and surely, in fairness to him, we should not overstate nor deify the coming of Obama. And yet, one really cannot overstate the significance of this event. Whatever Obama's legacy may be, his election as the first African-American president of the United States is, itself, historic and symbolic of an unshackling of vestiges of economic

[2] William Butler Yeats, *The Second Coming*, (Chicago: The Dial, 1920); (London: The Nation, 1929); in *Michael Robartes and the Dancer* (Dundrum: Cuala, 1921); in *Later Poems* (London: Macmillan, 1922; 1924; 1926; 1931).

and social discrimination.

And surely, Obama's election magnifies and adds to the democratic, egalitarian ethic found in the credo of the United States and manifested, poetically and prosaically, through recollections of Lincoln's commitment to Emancipation, the Suffrage movement, Franklin Roosevelt's advocacy for the rights of labor, and the two decades post-WWII that witnessed not just a Jackie Robinson, but *Brown v. Board of Education*, and the Civil Rights Act.

What might all of this mean for higher education? The significance of a waxing egalitarian ethic prompted by the Obama election will enrich the longstanding debate over whether higher education is a resource for the wealthy or a communal resource fundamentally important to sustain America's place in the world. To the extent an election signals a mandate for a President to remedy roots of adversity in his (or, someday, her) own life, one has to predict that the next four years, or more, will be characterized by national efforts to ensure that education, to include higher education, will be viewed as a moral imperative for all.

Of course, the ideological assumption that education, like health care, is a fundamental human right and social imperative will be challenged as a global recession, core industry disruptions, calls for universal health care, geo-political conflict, excessive national debt, and a rise in the cost of college relative to family incomes—even with increased student aid—become more evident through the course of Obama's first term. Paradoxically, however, it may be exactly such a "perfect storm" that renders the debate over whether education is a special interest versus fundamentally important national asset, moot and supportive of the latter assumption.

Second, and flowing from the first, is our founding propensity to continue to minimize, if not virtually eliminate, the place of aristocracy over meritocracy in our lives. Of course, the current push for meritocracy over aristocracy may represent a short-lived response to the George W. Bush legacy. And, as with most ideological advocacy, the push for meritocracy over aristocracy may be so forcefully evident today that it has already emerged in fanciful and extreme forms—to wit, the 2008 U.S. national election and the McCain campaign's flawed reach to "everyman" in the form of Sarah Palin and "Joe the Plumber"—even to such extent that the historically egalitarian, pro-meritocracy Democratic Party's countervailing response to McCain's claimed alliance with the ordinary citizen seemed oddly elitist. And, on a more popular plane, consider the 2009 award-winning film *Slum Dog Millionaire* and its dramatization of our faulty tendency to assume that knowledge flows from aristocratic bounty and not from the chaotic lives of the uneducated, unendowed underclass.

But, assuming the push for meritocracy over aristocracy is sustained, what is its significance to higher education? The consequence to higher education of a bias toward merit over social standing is likely to emerge in ways that challenge prior assumptions of curriculum design, performance measures, and the relevance of native intelligence and talent. What is likely to occur is not simply a reiteration of the debate over the importance of "soft skills" versus "hard skills," or C.P. Snow's "Two Cultures,"[3] but a market demand for college graduates able to demonstrate both.

One response to the call for "hard skills," and the ability to perform, is likely to result in the increased acceptance of such experiential learning methodologies as internships, travel, internet-based simulations, and a greater use of group-centered learning—and all linked, perhaps, to a broadly sculpted form of national service. Indeed, the call for colleges to develop not just a credentialed citizenry, but one capable of high performance and execution, seems to be growing louder. Increased global competitiveness, economic pressures and greater demands for economic returns on college investment, heightened concern for environmental preservation, and recent history suggesting that the "smartest guys in the room" aren't always the most effective nor most ethical performers, all argue for colleges to develop people who can *perform* effectively and morally.

Notably, a more forceful call for performance over pedigree

---

[3] C.P. Snow, "Two Cultures," *Science* 130, no. 3373 (1959): 419.

or credential is evidenced in the popular press. Consider, for example, the often cited controversial Charles Murray who claims that college is a "waste of time" for most students and that we should not be lulled into thinking that just because a person graduated from college, even a "prestigious college," they are prepared to bring value to the world of markets and geo-politics. Rather, Murray urges, we should independently test and certify the ability to perform and not rely merely on the assumption that a college degree means one is able to perform.[4] Add such popular and professional rhetoric as that coming from Malcolm Gladwell, Geoff Colvin, and, earlier, Henry Mintzberg, and what begins to emerge is a waning regard for both traditional aristocracy and a socially engineered and credentialed elite emanating from the "best" colleges and universities.[5]

In all of this, it is important to recall that much of American higher education was developed in concert with the Industrial Revolution and the formation of present-day corporations. Colleges and universities, especially through the 20th century, have been the source of talent for economic, social, and political systems that, for the most part, have evidenced a reasonably defined, stable, and successful existence.

But, today's organizations, from General Motors to Verizon to Microsoft and Google, are in the midst of market and organizational transformations in ways yet to be defined. The significance to higher education is that the demand for human talent honed by prescribed educational systems responsive to well-defined organizational needs, is likely to yield to a demand for "seers," entrepreneurs, and other organizational visionaries who can pave new paths.[6] Again, higher education's next

---

[4] Charles Murray, "For Most People, College is a Waste of Time," *Wall Street Journal*, 13 August 2008, U.S. ed., A17; Charles Murray, "Should the Obama Generation Drop Out?" *New York Times*, 28 December 2008, New York ed., WK9.

[5] Malcolm Gladwell, *Outliers: The Story of Success*, (New York: Little Brown and Company, 2008); Geoff Colvin, *Talent is Overrated: What Really Separates World-Class Performers from Everybody Else* (New York: Portfolio, 2008); Henry Mintzberg, "Musings on Management," *Harvard Business Review* 74, no. 4 (1996): 61-67.

[6] Contemporary history, especially as it relates to the "Information Age," is filled with heroic stories of entrepreneurship on the part of individuals who

generation will be called upon to do more than merely credential those with native intelligence; rather, higher education will be beckoned to energize and synergize habits of the mind along with a creative pragmatism necessary for innovation and competition in an increasingly complex world.

Homage to egalitarianism and meritocracy over aristocracy is so imbued into the fabric of our national credo that discourse on such ideals is often laced with inspirational platitudes that threaten to dilute the message. Such risk is equally apparent with the third force likely to shape the future of higher education: that of an enhanced facility to access information. Such condition is evidenced not only by an omnipresence of information technology, but by an abundance of books and blogs, which bugle the power of IT.[7]

The business world is embraced in a "love-hate" relationship with the likes of Google. On the one hand, businesses are dependent upon the power of Google-like search engines; on the other, the more sophisticated such systems become, the more the traditional corporate world, especially the consumer products world, fears it is witnessing the end of an era in the way businesses and other forms of organization are operated.

What sophisticated search engines portend is the delivery of "perfect information." Even those with a most basic understanding of microeconomic markets know that firms profit not from markets characterized by complete and symmetric information, but rather from imperfect and asymmetric market information. Competitive advantage is gained traditionally from the market's *perception* of value shaped by brand-building, advertising, and other such influences crafted by powerful organizations; it is not reaped from taking pains to construct a fully informed marketplace.

For example, imagine a world where one's search for the "perfect purchase"—one which actually assures the best quality at the lowest price based on a "perfect information system"— is available at the click of a mouse. Such a world would be

never earned a college degree. Bill Gates (Microsoft), Steven Jobs (Apple), and Michael Dell (Dell Computers) come to mind.

[7] Most recognized, of course, is Thomas Friedman's *The World is Flat* (New York: Farrar, Straus, & Giroux, 2005).

essentially devoid of competitive advantage flowing solely from an organization's ability to shape consumer perception. In fact, such a world would essentially shift the balance of economic power from vendors to consumers and in doing so would render the classic caution, *caveat emptor*, obsolete.

Interestingly, higher education's historic appeal, too, has been founded more on imperfect information and an aura of mystery rather than upon a fully informed user public. Public perception of higher education's early institutions was soothed by unquestioned faith given that many institutions were governed by religious founders who, rightly or wrongly, reaped public confidence. In time, public confidence in academia was also fostered by the arrival of public institutions built on a legal platform of public interest and disclosure.

In addition, parental participation in the college experience was much more distant until the latter part of the 20th century, especially for parents who had never attended college or possessed limited mobility. Paradoxically, an incomplete understanding of the academy, abetted by unfamiliar traditions rooted in medieval vestiges of the Renaissance, served to *heighten* parental and student trust in the academy—a clear example of the curious correlation between mystery and prestige.

Such was the case with my parents, neither college graduates, who drove me an hour to New York City, where I boarded a bus at Rockefeller Center en route to Hoboken, where I boarded an Erie Railroad train for a 300-mile trip to a college I then saw for the first time, suitcase and college catalog in hand, with confidence in my choice derived from faith in the university's historical repertoire and the testimony of guidance counselors and alumni. Four years later, my parents visited for the first time to witness my graduation.

As today's more college-educated "helicopter" parents and seemingly more parent-connected high school students engage the college selection process armed with more informed insight into the college choice question, the mystical character of higher education is clearly diminished. Sadly, however, in its place is a more synthetic measure of value and "prestige" formed by journalistic rankings, athletic prowess, facilities which rival the best country clubs, and costly branding and marketing strategies—all of which combine to epitomize a dramatic disclosure of the etymology of the word "prestige" as derived from the Latin, *praestigium*, meaning magic, illusion, trickery, sleight of hand. . . .

For many, the lure of college with its often-genuine promise of social certification, newly found independence, and promise of life-long professional and personal relationships, will remain understandably unquestioned. If, however, forecasters are correct in predicting declines in both family income and public support relative to increasing college costs, the consequence will be greater price sensitivity among families and legislatures, greater reluctance to assume that high price equates with high quality, and a clarion call for accountability and educational reform.

Moreover, our "Google society," fueled by a search for "truth" and full disclosure resulting from the costly absence of such qualities in the Enron-centric markets of the '90s and again by the financial crisis of 2008, is likely to call upon higher education for more *information*, not persuasion, as evidence of value. Such prediction should not come as a surprise to the higher education community; accrediting agencies have routinely demanded more and more "assessment" data. For years, many have urged the academy to take the lead in formulating and disclosing standardized performance metrics in much the same way publicly held, for-profit organizations are required to reveal financial performance based upon generally accepted accounting principles—imperfect as they may be.[8]

Some may lament a mechanistic drift toward fact-based outcomes assessment as an unfortunate departure from the more poetic appeals of *alma mater*, historical repertoire, institutional lore, and inspirational credo. In response, one can only note that colleges and universities need not forego the place of credo as a measure of distinction and distinctiveness, but rather strive to ensure a match between credo and credibility; for an "industry"

[8] Elizabeth M. Farrell and Martin Van Der Werf. "Playing the Rankings Game," *The Chronicle of Higher Education*, 25 May 2007, A11; Joseph M. Pastore, Jr., "Developing an Academic Accreditation Process Relevant to the Accounting Profession," *The CPA Journal* 159, no. 3 (1989): 18-26.

whose "core business" is the search for truth, we should expect nothing less.

REFLECTION

Musing on the future of anything is often fraught with error. Wasn't it John Lennon who wrote: "Life is what happens. . .when you are making other plans"?

Prudence dictates that higher education has little choice but to scan its environment and craft a future. Surely, dramatic transformations, indeed creative destructions, of some of our most traditional institutions and conventions—spurred by market forces, symbolic political shifts, disruptive technology, ethical breaches, more informed markets, and calls for greater access by historically marginalized segments of our society— should prompt studied pause among higher education leaders, to include trustees and other overseers responsible for ensuring a sustainable future for their institutions. Such pause will require a measured preservation of the past along with the strength and willingness to imagine a new order for the future.

Despite its title, this piece may be less about predicting the future of higher education and more about gently suggesting that the professional life of John Cronin may serve as a metaphor for the reform of higher education. What John has done as a beacon of change in the way we view our natural resources, especially water, could be done only by someone who is sufficiently courageous—even presumptuous—to see and accept things not as they are, but as they should be. John's values and work ethic call to mind Ursula Le Guin's fictional city of Omelas and some of its inhabitants who came to realize what they once perceived to be a utopian community awash in happiness was, instead, one in which happiness came at an unbearable human cost to those without voice. Thus, they chose to be "the ones that walk away. . ." and, metaphorically, I think John may have been among them.[9]

In all of this, one thing is clear. John's achievements were

---

[9] Ursula K. Le Guin, "The Ones Who Walk Away from Omelas," in *The Wind's Twelve Quarters: Short Stories* (New York: Harper & Row, 1975).

harvested not in spite of his non-traditional formation, but as a *result* of such formation. There may be a lesson in that for the future of higher education.

ABOUT THE AUTHORS

GEORGE ANCONA——I grew up in Coney Island, New York. Both my parents came from Yucatan in Mexico. My father came to study accounting; my mother came to visit her two brothers. That's where they met. They fell in love, got married, and I was born.

When I was twelve, I began to work after school; first for an auto mechanic, and then at the Spook House. In junior high, I discovered type in my sign painting class.

In high school, I studied graphic design and took Saturday classes at the Brooklyn Museum Art School where I met Rufino Tamayo. Immediately after graduation, I boarded a Greyhound bus for Mexico City. There Maestro Tamayo arranged for me to study at the Academia de San Carlos. After a few months, I left to go to Yucatan to meet my parents' families.

After six months in Mexico, I returned to New York to work and take up a scholarship to the Art Students League. I also studied at Cooper Union night school. During the day, I entered the world of publishing as an apprentice, then a designer and finally an art director for *Esquire, Seventeen Magazine*, and then for advertising agencies.

During these ten years, I married, had three children and began to photograph them. As an art director, I noticed that the photographers I contracted with were having more fun than I. It was then that I decided to leave my job to become a free-lance photographer.

My photographs began to be published in magazines and advertising. Eventually, I began to produce films. I did several documentaries for *Sesame Street* and other clients.

A friend who wrote children's books suggested that we try doing a book together. I found the experience very gratifying and began to photograph more books. My editor suggested I try writing. I did and the book was published. Today, I use words to convey what the pictures cannot say.

Twenty years ago we left New York and moved to Santa Fe, New Mexico. I went there to do a book and was attracted by an adobe studio with an attached one-room house. Later, we built a larger house nearby. Now we have room for the six children, four grandchildren, and three great-grandchildren to stay when they visit.

To create a book, I meet people who open their lives to me. Then I return to my studio where I put the book together; words, pictures, and design. For me, books are my way of sharing the experiences that have become a part of my life. I've just finished my 113th book.

In my way, I try to do what my father did when he would take me by the hand to walk the docks of Brooklyn looking up at the huge black hulls of freighters from all over the world. I became aware that there are far away places and people that some day I would get to know. I try to do this for children with my books.

GEOFFREY L. BRACKETT——Geoffrey L. Brackett is Provost and Executive Vice President for Academic Affairs at Pace University. After completing his undergraduate studies at DePauw University, Geoff earned his DPhil in English Literature at the University of Oxford. During his 19 years at Pace, he has served the University in many capacities, most recently as associate provost for Academic Affairs, from 2006–2007 and chairman of the Department of English in the Dyson Colleges of Arts and Sciences from 2005–2006.

A member of the Modern Language Association, the Northeast Society for Eighteenth Century Studies, and the North American Society for the Study of Romanticism, Geoff has represented Pace at numerous conferences. He was recently invited to speak at the American Museum of Natural History during the New York City International Polar Weekend on the importance of the literary understanding of the polar regions in the context of environmental awareness. As a member of the Environmental Consortium of Hudson Valley Colleges and Universities, Geoff has developed curriculum for its River Summer program in collaboration with colleagues from Columbia, Barnard, Vassar, Skidmore and other Hudson River institutions. He authored and presented "The Poet Speaks of Rivers: Place, Rivers and the Urban Dilemma" published in *Proceedings from the Pace Institute for Environmental and Regional Studies, Volume 4* (2004), 67-81. He has presented in many conferences on literature from the Romantic Period through the Beat Generation throughout his academic career.

Geoff has been twice recognized for his outstanding teaching by Dyson College. He is currently editing a textbook of collected writings about aesthetics, literature, and environmental studies entitled *The Hudson River and the American Tide: A Reader*, which grew out of courses taught at Pace, and has recently completed a travel memoir about his trips to Alaska and Antarctica, *Occidental Traveler*. Beyond his academic achievements, Geoff is a songwriter and a musician and member of Broadcast Music, Inc.

PAUL M. BRAY——Paul M. Bray is an attorney and graduate from Columbia University School of Law. He is associate counsel at New York State Department of Environmental Conservation and member of the Commissioner's Policy Office. He also is a lecturer in the Department of Geography and Planning at the University at Albany and editor of *Capital Commons Quarterly: The Dynamics of Aging and Our Communities* and a monthly columnist with the *Times Union* in Albany. He was senior counsel with the NYS Legislative Bill Drafting Commission and was Congressman Maurice Hinchey's bill drafter when Hinchey was a member of the NYS Assembly. Bray was a recipient of the Rome Prize from the American Academy in Rome for his park and conservation work and was honored by the New York State Bar Association Environmental Section ("For craftsmanship in the development of environmental legislation in New York

State").

MARY G. BURNS——Mary G. Burns is an Archaeological Consultant working on preservation issues in the mid-Hudson region. After writing a thesis regarding the looting of Magdalen Island in the Tivoli Bays area, she received a Masters of Science in Environmental Studies (MSES) at Bard College in 1998. Since then, she has voluntarily worked to protect that site as well as other looted archaeological sites on New York State land. She previously worked for over twenty years in the publishing industry.

ANTHONY DEPALMA——Anthony DePalma was the first foreign correspondent of the *New York Times* to serve as bureau chief in both Mexico and Canada. Starting in 1993, he covered some of the most tumultuous events in modern Mexican history, including the Zapatista uprising, the assassination of the ruling party's presidential candidate and the peso crisis that quickly spread economic chaos to markets all over the world. In 1996 he was transferred to Canada, where he reported from all ten provinces and three territories, including the new territory of Nunavut, in which Inuit people formed their own government.

Besides North America, DePalma has reported from Cuba, Guatemala, Suriname, Guyana, and, during the Kosovo crisis, Montenegro and Albania. His book *Here: A Biography of the New American Continent*, was published in the United States and Canada in 2001. An updated version, with a post 9/11 afterword, was published in 2002. He wrote nearly 100 of the Portraits of Grief about 9/11 victims that won the Pulitzer Prize.

From 2000 to 2002, DePalma was an international business correspondent for the *New York Times* covering North and South America. During his tenure with the *Times*, he also has held positions in the Metropolitan and National sections of the newspaper. Most recently he wrote about the environment. In 2003, he was awarded a fellowship at Notre Dame's Kellogg Institute for International Studies, where he began work on his book *The Man Who Invented Fidel*, published in 2006. It has been translated into Spanish, Portuguese and Italian, and has been optioned by a motion picture production company.

DePalma has taught graduate seminars at Columbia University and New York University. In 2007 he was named a Hoover Media Fellow at Stanford University, and he delivered the annual Jane E. Ruby Lecture at Wheaton College. He was nominated for a 2007 Emmy for his work on the television documentary "Toxic Legacy."

In September 2008, Mr. DePalma was named writer-in-residence at Seton Hall University. He is now writing a book on the health and environmental aftermath of the attack on the World Trade Center, the greatest environmental disaster in the history of New York.

JIM DETJEN——Jim Detjen holds the Knight Chair in Journalism and is the director of the Knight Center for Environmental Journalism at Michigan State University. During his 21-year career as an environmental journalist at the *Philadelphia Inquirer* and other newspapers he won more than 45 state and national journalism awards. He is now an award-winning educator who has trained thousands of students and journalists around the world to report and write about environmental issues.

ALEXANDRA DAPOLITO DUNN——Alexandra Dapolito Dunn is Assistant Dean for Environmental Law Programs and Adjunct Professor of Law (Environmental Justice, Human Rights and the Environment) at Pace University School of Law in White Plains, New York. She wanted to write for this publication because John Cronin is an inspirational individual who has made an immeasurable difference in the Hudson River's water quality and to her children's clean water future.

Dean Dunn oversees the Law School's environmental law programs and curriculum, consistently ranked among the top three in the nation. She focuses her research and policy work at Pace's *Center for Environmental Legal Studies* on climate change, water quality, green urbanism, open space and poverty, and sustainability. Dunn serves as Curriculum Advisor to Pace Law's *Theodore W. Kheel Center on the Resolution of Environmental Interest Disputes* and represents Pace Law School on the Steering Committee of the Environmental Consortium of Hudson Valley Colleges and Universities.

Dunn previously served as General Counsel of the National Association of Clean Water Agencies (NACWA) in Washington, D.C. Prior to NACWA, Dunn served as Counsel to the American Chemistry Council in Arlington, Virginia. She began her career in Washington, D.C. as an environmental associate at Winston & Strawn.

In her years of practice, Dunn represented parties, intervenors, or *amicus curiae* in over twenty-five environmental cases, including *National Ass'n of Home Builders v. Defenders of Wildlife*, 549 U.S. 1105 (2007); *Friends of the Earth v. EPA*, 446 F.3d 140 (D.C. Cir. 2006); *South Florida Water Management District v. Miccosukee Tribe of Indians*, 541 U.S. 95 (2004); *Friends of the Earth v. EPA*, 346 F. Supp.2d 182 (D.D.C. 2004); *Pennsylvania Municipal Authorities Ass'n v. Horinko*, 292 F. Supp.2d (D.D.C. 2003); *Ohio Valley Environmental Coalition v. Horinko*, 279 F. Supp.2d 732 (S.D.W.Va. 2003); *Whitman v. American Trucking Associations, Inc. et al.*, 531 U.S. 457 (2001); *Appalachian Power Co. v. EPA*, 208 F.3d 1015 (D.C. Cir. 2000); and *Clean Air Implementation Project v. EPA*, 150 F.3d 1200 (D.C. Cir. 1998).

Dunn serves as Education Officer for the American Bar Association's 11,000 member Section of Environment, Energy, and Resources. She is a member of the Environmental Law Committee of the Association of the Bar of the City of New York. She serves on the Board of Directors of the Clean Water America Alliance and is the community recruiter for the Ossining, New York Council of Girl Scouts of America.

She earned her Juris Doctor in 1994, *magna cum laude*, from the Columbus School of Law, Catholic University of America, where she served as Editor-in-Chief of the *Catholic University Law Review* and was selected as the *Outstanding Woman Law Graduate* and received a *Dean's Award* for *Dedicated Service to the Law School Community*. She earned her Bachelor of Arts in 1989, *cum laude*, in Political Science and French from James Madison University. Dunn is admitted to the District of Columbia, Maryland, and New York bars, the U.S. Supreme Court, and federal circuit and district courts.

STEPHEN J. FRIEDMAN——Stephen J. Friedman became the seventh president of Pace University on June 4, 2007. Friedman is a former senior partner at Debevoise & Plimpton LLC, commissioner of the Securities and Exchange Commission, deputy assistant secretary of the Treasury, executive vice president and general counsel at The Equitable Companies Incorporated and the E.F. Hutton Group Inc., and U.S. Supreme Court law clerk to Justice William J. Brennan Jr. (1963-1964).

Friedman served for three years as Dean of Pace University School of Law prior to being named president by the Pace University Board of Trustees.

Friedman is chairman emeritus of the American Ballet Theatre. He also serves as a trustee of the Commission on Independent Colleges and Universities, the Practising Law Institute, and serves on the Board of Directors for the Alliance for Downtown New York, Inc., the Westchester County Association, and Project Rebirth. Friedman is also a member of the Board of Trustees of The New York Downtown Hospital, the National Commission for Cooperative Education, and the Beacon Institute for Rivers and Estuaries.

Friedman received his AB *magna cum laude* in 1959 from the Woodrow Wilson School of Public and International Affairs at Princeton University, and his Juris Doctor *magna cum laude* in 1962 from Harvard Law School, where he was an editor of Harvard Law Review and a recipient of the Sears Prize.

JEFF GOLLIHER——The Rev. Canon Jeffrey Mark Golliher, Ph.D., cultural anthropologist and priest in the Episcopal Church, has traveled widely to understand the spiritual dimension of the environmental crisis. For over ten years, he was Canon for Environmental Justice and Community Development at the Cathedral of St. John the Divine and Manhattan. Today, he is a parish priest at St. John's Church in Ellenville, New York, a member of the Third Order of the Society of Saint Francis (TSSF), and a spiritual director, working with people who want to live in more spiritually-aware, healthy, and sustainable ways. As the environmental representative for the worldwide Anglican Communion at the United Nations, he has organized global conferences on spirituality, ecology, and community development, and he has written and edited numerous books and articles on these subjects for the church and the United Nations. His recent book, entitled *A Deeper Faith: A Journey into Spirituality*, was published by Tarcher/Penguin in 2008. He was born and raised in the Blue Ridge Mountains of western North Carolina. He currently lives with his wife, Asha, in upstate New York.

HENRY GOURDINE——The *New York Times* called Henry Gourdine "a Hudson River legend" and "a living museum." Governor George E. Pataki called him "a state treasure." Henry was also a commercial fisherman, net maker, boat builder, and carpenter. He was born in Croton-on-Hudson, New York and from a young age harbored an irrepressible attraction for the river and for fishing. He made it his business to learn every craft of the trade and by his twenties could build a commercial fishing operation from a pile of lumber and a mile of line.

Henry knew how to net and trap anything that swam—striped bass, American shad, carp, American eel, blue crab—and enjoyed ocean angling for tuna and bluefish. He had one of the largest shad fishing operations on the river, with a round-the-clock crew and a retired railroad barge for a bunkhouse. As much as he loved working from boats, Henry spoke longingly of his days as a haul-seiner for striped bass at Crawbuckie beach in the Village of Ossining. When the New York State legislature ended that practice on the Hudson, under pressure from the Long Island fishing industry, he developed a lifelong distrust of regulations and their enforcers.

Henry was as fond of fishing as he was of boasting his disgust with it. Reflecting on a particularly dismal season he said, "I had a mind to throw a pair of oars on my shoulder and just keep walking until someone said, 'What are those things?' And then that's where I'd stay." When asked why he kept fishing he replied, "I've got a strong back and a weak mind, I guess." His self-deprecation was a well-known trait that belied a deep wisdom about life on the Hudson, and life generally.

Henry took great pride in work and in passing his skills to eager students. He was a regular feature at riverside festivals where his trademark "Net Doctor" tool kit sat fast beside while he tutored young children in the delicate operation of sewing a net. Less obviously, Henry's talents were in demand by commercial fishermen as well. The late Tucker Crawford of Verplanck proudly fished from one of Henry's hand-built boats and relied on Henry to hang his sturgeon nets. He said, "There should be a commercial fishing school, and Henry should be the professor."

Henry died on October 17, 1997 at age ninety-four while working on nets in the basement of his home on Independence Avenue in Ossining. It was a measure of his vitality that all who knew him were shocked by the news. "Duty Bound" is taken from a recently found recorded interview conducted with Henry by John Cronin in summer 1982.

JIM HERON——Jim Heron serves as the Project Historian for Beacon Institute for Rivers and Estuaries. Following twenty-three years as rector of Trinity Episcopal Church in Fishkill, New York, he joined the staff of Beacon Institute in 2003. Jim began a second career at the Institute as the author of *Denning's Point, A Hudson River History* and offers public outreach presentations for Beacon Institute about the history of Denning's Point, Beacon, New York. Jim is a consummate story-teller and a popular public speaker. He has held teaching positions at both high school and college level institutions. His own never-ending education and that of students remains important; he earned his Bachelor of Arts degree from Norwich University, a Masters degree in Sacred Theology from the Episcopal Divinity School, and a Doctorate in Ministry from Drew University. Jim lives in Beacon and has two adult children living on the West Coast. He delights in a challenging project and has at least one ongoing at all times often finding intriguing ways of incorporating his hobbies which include photography, creating scroll saw art, mineralogy, and baseball. When Jim relaxes completely, it is by contemplating Sin (short for "Sinders," his ash-gray cat) in front of a glowing fire, mystery novel in hand, eagerly anticipating his next project...perhaps it will include the thrill of searching through more dusty archives to shed light on other real-life mysteries?

JOHN HORGAN——John Horgan is a freelance journalist who teaches and directs the Center for Science Writings at Stevens Institute of Technology, Hoboken, New Jersey. A former senior writer at *Scientific American* (1986-1997), he has also written for the *New York Times, National Geographic, Discover, Time, Newsweek*, the *Washington Post, Slate, New Scientist* and other publications around the world. His books include *The End of Science* (1996), *The Undiscovered Mind* (1999) and *Rational Mysticism* (2003). Horgan blogs at the website of the Center for Science Writings (stevens.edu/csw) and participates in the weekly "Science Saturday" show on *Bloggingheads.tv*. His awards include the Science Journalism Award of the American Association for the Advancement of Science and the National Association of Science Writers Science-in-Society Award. His articles are featured in the last three editions of *The Best American Science and Nature Writing*. Horgan graduated from the Columbia University School of Journalism in 1983. He lives in Cold Spring, New York.

ROBERT F. KENNEDY, JR.——Robert F. Kennedy, Jr.'s reputation as a resolute defender of the environment stems from a litany of successful legal actions. Kennedy was named one of Time magazine's "Heroes for the Planet" for his success helping Riverkeeper lead the fight to restore the Hudson River.

The group's achievement helped spawn over 185 Waterkeeper organizations across the globe.

Kennedy serves as Senior Attorney for the Natural Resources Defense Council, Chief Prosecuting Attorney for the Hudson Riverkeeper and Chairman of Waterkeeper Alliance. He is also a Clinical Professor and Supervising Attorney at Pace University School of Law's Environmental Litigation Clinic and is co-host of Ring of Fire on Air America Radio. Earlier in his career he served as Assistant District Attorney in New York City.

He has worked on environmental issues across the Americas and has assisted several indigenous tribes in Latin America and Canada in successfully negotiating treaties protecting traditional homelands. He is credited with leading the fight to protect New York City's water supply. The New York City watershed agreement, which he negotiated on behalf of environmentalists and New York City watershed consumers, is regarded as an international model in stakeholder consensus negotiations and sustainable development. He helped lead the fight to turn back the anti-environmental legislation during the 104th Congress.

Kennedy's published books include the *New York Times'* bestseller *Crimes Against Nature* (2004), *The Riverkeepers* (1997), co-authored by John Cronin, and *Judge Frank M. Johnson, Jr: A Biography* (1977) and two children's books *St Francis of Assisi* (2005), *American Heroes: Joshua Chamberlain and the American Civil War* and *Robert Smalls: The Boat Thief* (2008). His articles have appeared in the *New York Times, Washington Post, Los Angeles Times, Wall Street Journal, Newsweek, Rolling Stone, Atlantic Monthly, Esquire, The Nation, Outside* magazine, *The Village Voice,* and many other publications. His award-winning articles have been included in anthologies of America's Best Crime Writing, Best Political Writing and Best Science Writing.

Kennedy is a graduate of Harvard University. He studied at the London School of Economics and received his law degree from the University of Virginia Law School. Following graduation he attended Pace University School of Law, where he was awarded a Masters Degree in Environmental Law.

He is a licensed master falconer, and as often as possible he pursues a life-long enthusiasm for white-water paddling. He has organized and led several expeditions in Canada and Latin America, including first descents on three little-known rivers in Peru, Colombia, and Venezuela.

HARRY R. KOLAR——Harry R. Kolar is the Chief Architect for Sensor-Based Solutions and a Senior Technical Staff Member in the IBM Microelectronics Division of the Systems and Technology Group. Kolar concentrates on environmental monitoring and management through the IBM Big Green Innovations initiative within IBM's "Smarter Planet" program. His interests are focused in exploiting existing and emerging technologies for the next generation of intelligent systems for the environmental domain.

Kolar has worked across several IBM divisions in technical, management, and executive roles to advance cross-industry application of new technologies. These include advanced analytical methods (involving signal processing, data mining, massively parallel processors, and very large databases), information and knowledge management, pervasive and embedded real-time intelligent systems, and sensor-based/cyberphysical systems. He is the lead architect for IBM's SmartBay Galway project in collaboration with the Marine Institute of Ireland and a Cyber-Infrastructure Advisor for the Beacon Institute for Rivers and Estuaries' River and Estuary Observatory Network (REON). Kolar is also involved in the Science Foundation of Ireland's CLARITY Centre for Science, Engineering, and Technology (CSET) focused on sensor web technologies through the intersection of adaptive sensing and information discovery. CLARITY is a multidisciplinary partnership involving the University College Dublin, Dublin City University, and the Tyndall National Institute, Cork.

Kolar received BS and MS degrees in physics and an interdisciplinary PhD degree in the science and engineering of materials from Arizona State University. His research efforts focused on real-time *in-situ* atomic resolution imaging of defects in silicon. He joined IBM from Arizona State University where he coordinated external user research efforts for the National Science Foundation John M. Cowley Center for High Resolution Electron Microscopy. Kolar began his career with IBM in magnetoresistive and magneto-optical thin-film development at the IBM General Products Division laboratory in Tucson, Arizona. He was also an independent scientific consultant for the Atlantic Richfield Company Advanced Materials Development Laboratory in Chatsworth, California. Kolar is an Adjunct Professor of Physics at Arizona State University and a District Advocate for the American Physical Society at the U.S. congressional level.

MICHELLE D. LAND——Michelle D. Land is the Director of Pace University's Academy for Applied Environmental Studies. She also directs the Environmental Consortium of Hudson Valley Colleges and Universities, hosted by Pace.

Land lectures regionally and nationally on environmental policy and ecosystem-based higher education, and is an advisor on regional climate change mitigation. She is an Adjunct Associate Professor in the graduate environmental science program at Pace, and teaches graduate environmental policy at New York University. Land is also the co-chair of Pace University's Sustainability Committee.

Prior to her current position, Land was Program Coordinator of Pace Academy for the Environment from its inception in 2002 until it morphed into the new Academy. Land's previous career in wildlife biology at the World Bird Sanctuary in St. Louis, Missouri, included field studies, education programs, propagation, rehabilitation, and release of endangered birds of prey.

Land represents Pace University on the national Council of Environmental Deans and Directors. She was appointed by Westchester County Executive Andrew Spano to the Global Warming Task Force in 2007, and serves on his Climate Change Advisory Council as chair of the Higher Education Sector. She is an advisor on higher education to the Beacon Institute for Rivers and Estuaries, and is an executive member of the Board of Directors for MetroPool, Inc., a non-profit organization that fosters solutions for transportation demand management.

Land received her Juris Doctor from Pace University School of Law, where she earned a certificate in environmental law and served as Editor-in-Chief of the Pace Environmental Law Review. She earned her Bachelor of Science degree with a specialty in wildlife biology from the Honours Program at the University of Guelph in Ontario, Canada, and she has undertaken masters-level study in ecology at the University of Missouri-St. Louis.

Currently, Land's areas of research interest include the intersection of nanotechnology regulation, environment and ethics as well as animal welfare and conservation policy.

JOSEPH M. PASTORE, JR.——Joseph M. Pastore, Jr., is Professor Emeritus (in Residence), Lubin School of Business, Pace University. He holds degrees from St. Bonaventure University, Pace University, and Saint Louis University and he has engaged extended non-degree programs through Cornell University (1971-72) and Harvard University (Summer 1975).

Pastore has held tenured faculty appointments at St. Bonaventure University, Pace University, and Boston College. In addition, he has served as a Dean, Provost, and/or Executive Vice President for each of those institutions over a 23-year period. In 1988, Pastore was a Visiting Scholar at the Graduate School of Business, Columbia University.

Beyond teaching, Pastore has authored, co-authored, or edited over forty articles, monographs, papers, and book chapters in addition to scores of presentations at professional conferences and symposia. He has also lectured in executive development programs for such organizations as Verizon Communications, British Telecommunications, AT&T, Swiss Re, Monsanto, IBM, Prudential-Bache Securities, Technicon, Corning, Reader's Digest, and Dresser Industries.

Much of Pastore's professional life, beyond academia, has been devoted to dispute resolution. Pastore has served on the arbitration panels of the American Arbitration Association and Federal Mediation and Conciliation Service; his mediation and facilitation work included an on-going appointment by the U.S. District Court (Southern District) as Monitor and Special Master overseeing the Order to Desegregate the Yonkers Public Schools, Yonkers, New York. He is credited with mediating a $300 million settlement of that case, thereby concluding twenty years of litigation.

Pastore has also consulted and offered facilitation services for tens of non-profit organizations and his work in social entrepreneurship has been supported by grants from such sources as the Coleman Foundation, the Kauffman Foundation, the Carlisle Foundation, and various corporate foundations.

Pastore has been active in a variety of community and professional organizations to include membership on the Alumni Council of the Institute for Educational Management at Harvard University; as a Trustee of Siena College (Chair of the Board: 2004-2007); as a member of the Bucknell University Business Advisory Board; as a member of the President's Council, Northern Westchester Hospital Center; and, as a member of the Board of Directors for Abbott House, a child care agency in Irvington, N.Y.

He resides in Briarcliff Manor, New York with his wife, Pattie. They have three adult children and seven grandchildren.

Joseph Pastore wishes to express his gratitude to John Cronin for the non-traditional and exemplary professional life that John has embraced for decades and for the inspiration John's work provided for "Musings on the Future of Higher Education." John's work has served to call important attention to diverse patterns of learning, ranging from highly structured and institutionalized methodology to, as in John's case, creative and auto-didactic experiences. John's professional work has also provided a dose of humility for the academe, which can only help to ensure that the future of higher education remains promising.

NICHOLAS A. ROBINSON——Nicholas A. Robinson holds the esteemed position of University Professor at Pace University. He is the Gilbert & Sarah Kerlin Distinguished Professor of Environmental Law at Pace Law School, and a Professor Adjunct at the Yale University School of Forestry and Environmental Studies. He founded the internationally respected environmental law program at Pace Law School in 1978.

A specialist in comparative environmental law and environmental impact assessment, Robinson is engaged in research and capacity building in Asia, Africa and the Middle East. He serves on the Environmental and Social Advisory Committee for the European Bank for Reconstruction & Development in London. He has served as Deputy Commissioner and General Counsel of the New York State Department of Environmental Conservation, and authored the New York Tidal Wetlands Act and much of its Freshwater Wetlands, along with other laws and regulations.

Robinson was Legal Advisor to the International Union for the Conservation of Nature & Natural Resources (IUCN), and led the Asian Development Bank's programs to build capacity for research and teaching of environmental law throughout the Asian and Pacific Region. He co-edited the United Nations Environment Programme's Manual on International Environmental Law. He holds his Juris Doctor from Columbia University and his AB from Brown University.

SUSAN FOX ROGERS——Susan Fox Rogers is the editor of

eleven book anthologies, including *Solo: On her Own Adventure* (1996, 2005), *Going Alone: Women's Adventures in the Wild* (2004), and *Alaska Passages: 20 Voices from Above the 54th Parallel* (1996). In 2004-05, she traveled to Antarctica on a National Science Foundation grant and produced her most recent collection, *Antarctica: Life on the Ice* (2007), which won a silver medal in 2008 from the Society of American Travel Writers.

She is Visiting Associate Professor at Bard College, where she teaches creative writing and the First Year Seminar. She also teaches courses on Nature Writing and on the Hudson River Valley. Recently, she completed a book on the Hudson River from the perspective of her kayak titled *My Reach: Love and Loss on the Hudson River*. Chapters have been published in *Isotope: A Journal of Literary Nature and Science Writing, Under the Sun* and *Alaska Quarterly Review*. "Learning the River" is also taken from this longer work.

PETE SEEGER——Pete Seeger has spent his life singing for change—in the labor movement, the civil rights movement, the peace and anti-war movements, and the environmental movement. He helped to found the Hudson River Sloop Clearwater in 1966. The sloop Clearwater—a replica of the ships that sailed the Hudson in the 18th and 19th centuries—sails the river, fighting pollution and educating young and old about the environment. While Seeger was repairing the dock in Beacon, a fortuitous meeting with John Cronin inspired a 35-year career in environmental protection.

ALEC WILKINSON——Alec Wilkinson has been a writer at *The New Yorker* since 1980. Before that he was a policeman in Wellfleet, Massachusetts, and before that he was a rock-and-roll musician. His honors include a Guggenheim Fellowship, a Lyndhurst Prize, and a Robert F. Kennedy Book Award. He is the author of nine books, the most recent of which, *The Protest Singer*, about Pete Seeger, was released in 2009. John Cronin was the first person he wrote a Profile of; the piece appeared in the issue of *The New Yorker* for May 11, 1987, and is included in

Wilkinson's collection *The Riverkeeper* (1991).

ANDREW J. WILLNER——Andrew Willner has been a city planner, furniture designer, sculptor, boat builder, environmentalist, storyteller, and photographer. He was Executive Director and Baykeeper at NY/NJ Baykeeper for nineteen years and retired in April 2008.

He has started a consulting firm, Andrew J. Willner, Inc., is exhibiting and published a book of his photographs, and is a visiting public scholar at Monmouth University's Urban Coast Institute. He is a founding member and continues to serve on the international Waterkeeper Alliance Board of Directors and has traveled nationally and internationally to speak on behalf of the Waterkeeper model of water and habitat protection.

Mr. Willner is a sought-after speaker on a wide variety of subjects including environmental advocacy, habitat restoration, and sustainability. He is also called on to read from fiction and non-fiction works in progress, often supported by exhibitions of his photographs.

ACKNOWLEDGEMENTS

We are deeply grateful to the authors herein—an extraordinary group of people who gave generously of their time, talent and expertise.

Without the support, commitment, and advice of Provost Geoff Brackett, this book would not have been possible.

Our appreciation to Sasha Harris-Cronin for taking our vague ideas and turning them into magnificent book cover and table of contents designs.

The title of this book is taken—gleefully—from one of John Cronin's essays posted on www.johncronin.net.

Michelle Land would like to thank her husband and son for their kind understanding of the long hours this project required. Michelle also wishes to express gratitude to her proofreaders, Donna Kowal, Cecelia Land, and Kevin Winn for their keen eye in identifying errors and improving the flow of her Introduction.

Finally, a sincere thanks to the Pace University Press, especially graduate assistants Kristen Tomaiolo and Anjuli Lochan for their guidance and infinite patience.

Breinigsville, PA USA
24 November 2009
228094BV00002B/1/P